The Power of Worship

BY
CHRISTOPHER MONAGHAN

acknowledgements

I want to acknowledge my good friend and mentor, Todd Westphal. Thank you for always believing in me and encouraging me to go for more of Jesus in worship. You are to me, like Jonathan was to David. I dedicate this book to you because you model a heart of worship.

Thank you to Mary O'Neal and Gayla Meredith for their countless hours editing and formatting this work. Thank you also to Dr. Leon Van Rooyen for encouraging me to write about worship for Global Ministries Bible Institute. Because of your suggestion, *The Power of Worship* has become a reality.

CONTENTS

Chapter 1
Overcoming Worship!

"May the praise of God be in their mouths and a double-edged sword in their hands."

(Psalm 149:6)

W orship gives us the ability to enter into a heavenly realm where we gain strength, confidence and vision to overcome the challenges we face in the earthly realm. The praise of God in our mouths is like a double-edged sword through which we conquer our enemies. I am not implying that we ever focus on demons and Satan as we worship, but it is in darkness when we flip the light switch. The light switch represents giving adoration to our Heavenly Father and His Son, Jesus Christ.

As His presence descends, it crushes my enemies like a tin can in a metal press!

Character is produced as we worship because we are persevering in our declaration of God's goodness no matter what we face here on planet earth. The result of pressing into God's presence releases joy, maturity, wholeness, and complete provision. James declared in his letter:

Consider it pure joy, my brothers, whenever you face trials of many kinds, because you know that the testing of your faith develops perseverance. Perseverance must finish its work so that you may be mature and complete, not lacking anything.
(James 1:2-4)

Don't Let A Shot In The Chest Stop You!

Teddy Roosevelt served as the 26th president of the United States and was well known for his bold leadership. History records that as he was getting ready to speak while campaigning in Milwaukee, Wisconsin, in 1912, a saloonkeeper shot him in the chest. An experienced hunter, Roosevelt knew that, although the bullet was lodged in his chest, as long as he wasn't coughing up blood, he would be OK to speak as scheduled. He knew that if the bullet hadn't reached his lung, he had no immediate reason to go to the hospital. X-rays would later show that the bullet had penetrated three inches of tissue and had lodged in Roosevelt's chest muscle.

Few of us would have even remotely considered doing anything else but rushing immediately to the hospital. Not Teddy Roosevelt! With his knowledge of the human body and his determined leadership, not even a bullet to the chest could stop him from moving forward! This story gives me strength to pass on word to all who desire to stand before the LORD and minister. Don't let a mere shot to the chest stop you!

I have had the honor to be a leader in worship for almost 25 years at the time of this writing. My journey has been filled with seasons of ecstatic joy and seasons of pain and difficulty. In the past, I had fallen ill from the rejection of man, but now I have developed immunities to both the praises and rejection of man, enabling me to be free of the fear of man. Those seasons of rejection allow us to find our source of strength in God. Proverbs 29:25 warns us that, *"Fear of man will prove to be a snare."* We must not be like the religious leaders of Jesus' day who, *"...loved praise from men more than praise from God."* (John 12:43)

The message I want to share in this writing is the great power given to us through our worship. I pray you will walk in the same boldness that Teddy Roosevelt did throughout his life. You will experience pain in this life but you can also experience the power that flows through a worshipping heart. The scripture that has been the foundation of my life is found in Romans 12:11-12.

Never be lacking in zeal but keep your spiritual fervor serving the LORD. Be joyful in hope, patient in affliction, and faithful in prayer.

Throughout this book I want to give you a perspective needed to see the body of Christ plugged in to the power of worship. Joyful perseverance is needed if we are going to bring heaven to earth in our communities. Teddy Roosevelt's story reminds us that as we go about the work of God, there will be attacks and there will be opposition. Paul wrote to the Christians in Ephesus:

In addition to all this, take up the shield of faith, with which you can extinguish all the flaming arrows of the evil one.
(Ephesians 6:16)

Roosevelt miraculously survived the shot to his chest because the bullet was blocked by his steel eyeglass case and a thick, fifty-paged single-folded copy of the speech he was carrying in his jacket. The bullet had limited impact because it had to travel through these two items that I believe carry significant meaning.

Having A Vision To Worship

Roosevelt's steel eyeglass case represents his solid vision; if you have vision, you can persevere in just about anything. Responding to God in worship requires such vision; it must not be just an act of emotion: it must be an act of devotion. Experiencing worship will lift you out of your current situation into a place of power that must cover your heart at all times.

King David experienced the protection and comfort released through singing songs of deliverance! *"You are my hiding place; you will protect me from trouble and surround me with songs of deliverance"* (Psalm 32:7).

I can remember a season in my own life when I had been betrayed and watched everything around me falling apart. Looking back, I appreciate the ability I had to declare God's goodness as I listened to song after song declaring my breakthrough even though I felt like giving up and throwing in the towel! Worship pulls down the reality of your situation from God's perspective. Nothing that happens here on earth can cause fear on the throne of God. Paul said to the Ephesians, *"God raised us up with Christ and seated us with him in the heavenly realms in Christ Jesus"* (Ephesians 2:6).

The other object that hindered the bullet from hitting his heart was a fifty page folded copy of his speech. The number fifty represents the outpouring of the Holy Spirit. There are exactly fifty days between the feast of First fruits, when Jesus was risen, and the feast of Pentecost, when the Holy Spirit was poured out. We read about what happened to the disciples exactly fifty days after the resurrection of Christ: *"When the day of Pentecost came, they were all together in one place... all of them were filled with the Holy Spirit..."* (Acts 2:1,4).

The enemy's bullets are stopped by the shield created by the words of God that have flowed into our hearts through the Holy Spirit. Often these words come sung not spoken! Declaring the reality of who God is and how great His love is for us is one of the greatest tools we have in spiritual warfare!

Teddy Roosevelt addressed the gathered crowd, opening with the comment, **"Ladies and gentlemen, I don't know whether you fully understand that I have just been shot; but it takes more than that to kill a Bull Moose".** Roosevelt went on to speak for ninety minutes that day but he carried that bullet in his chest for the rest of his life.

The Power of Worship is written for anyone who seeks to bring the atmosphere of heaven to earth. This book is more of a straightforward, go-for-it message to a believer to worship than a critique of why power is not flowing. I believe success is 10% talent plus 90% passion for God not 90% talent with 10% passion for God.

Declaring God's Enduring Love

When a king of Israel was being brought into battle against three different nations, he placed the worship leaders in the frontlines! Every victory against our enemies begins with exalting the King of the Universe. It is time that worshippers arise and step into the front of the army.

Jehoshaphat appointed men to sing to the LORD and to praise him for the splendor of his holiness as they went out at the head of the army, saying: "Give thanks to the Lord, for his love endures forever." As they began to sing and praise, the Lord set ambushes against the men of Ammon and Moab and Mount Seir who were invading Judah, and they were defeated.

9

(2 Chronicles 20:21-22)

Victory was brought about as the Lord ambushed the enemies of Jehoshapat in the midst of their praise. They declared, *"Give thanks to the LORD, for His love endures forever!"* The word for love in this verse is the word *hesed*. *Hesed* is one of the most important words in the Hebraic Scriptures, meaning *"mercy, love, kindness, faithfulness."* The word is often translated *"steadfast love"*. One scholar described *hesed* as an act of God toward man.

An act of 'hesed' presupposes the existence of relationship between two parties involved, but where no formal relationship has previously been recognized, the person exercising 'hesed' has chosen to treat the recipient as if such a relationship did exist.[1]

I prefer to define *hesed* as covenant love. Covenants are commitments that are made with not only words, but with sacred oaths and the shedding of blood. The closest picture of covenant found in today's society is a wedding ceremony. Ancients would often 'cut' a covenant with another party by cutting an animal in half and walking between the two pieces of the butchered animal declaring, "May I become like this animal if I ever violate the terms of our agreement." *Hesed* is the love the flows out of this type of commitment.

We declare, "His *hesed* endures forever!" Jesus has brought us into covenant through His blood and our praise is now based upon His steadfast love toward us. As we worship, we are empowered by *hesed* and not by the circumstances of our life because His love never fails.

---

[1] Zodhiates, Spiros, and John R. Kohlenberger. *The Hebrew-Greek Key Study Bible: New International Version*. Chattanooga, TN: AMG Pub., 1996. 1516

Worship Is Recognition

Recognizing what Jesus has done releases power into our lives to make us overcomers. Believing in Jesus releases a flow of living waters!

Whoever believes in me, as the Scripture has said, streams of living water will flow from within him." By this he meant the Spirit, whom those who believed in him were later to receive. Up to that time the Spirit had not been given, since Jesus had not yet been glorified. (John 7:38-39)

Jesus said that His glorification would release the gift of the Spirit. We can simplify the idea of glorification as meaning recognition. Recognition means *"the acknowledgment of something's existence, validity, or legality or appreciation or acclaim for an achievement, service, or ability."*[2] When we exalt Jesus and recognize Him for who He is even in the midst of trials, we receive the Spirit of God into our lives.

Christians need power, so Christians *must* worship. We must become risk takers in our worship and not let the flaming darts of the enemy stop our praise on earth. I am determined that my song will not end until it reaches the heart of God and I feel His Spirit flowing out of me like a stream.

The name Theodore means gift of God. Theodore Roosevelt's life and words are a gift to bring us courage for the days ahead. We live in a crucial time and must no longer allow the enemy to distract us and put us on the defensive. Christians must get in the game and play offense! We must push aside the negativity and press into Jesus. President Roosevelt left us with these valuable words:

---

[2] Ehrlich, Eugene. *Oxford American Dictionary*. New York: Oxford UP, 1980.

It is not the critic who counts; not the man who points out how the strong man stumbles, or where the doer of deeds could have done them better. The credit belongs to the man who is actually in the arena, whose face is marred by dust and sweat and blood; who strives valiantly; who errs, who comes short again and again, because there is no effort without error and shortcoming; but who does actually strive to do the deeds; who knows great enthusiasms, the great devotions; who spends himself in a worthy cause; who at the best knows in the end the triumph of high achievement, and who at the worst, if he fails, at least fails while daring greatly, so that his place shall never be with those cold and timid souls who neither know victory nor defeat.

— Theodore Roosevelt

I hope this book encourages you to stand up and minister to the God the Father and His Son Jesus Christ! Don't hold back or store up your worship for another day! Surround the throne of God with your praise. Lavish the LORD with glory due His name.

Reflection

1. What is developed in your life as you persevere? Do you persevere in your worship regardless of your preference?
2. Theodore Roosevelt is a great example of perseverance and character. Describe a time when you were required to persevere and the character that was developed in you.
3. Define the Hebrew word *hesed*.
4. King Jehoshapat put singers at the head of his army. How would you feel if you were asked to lead the army into battle with nothing more than a song to God?
5. Do you have a vision and mission statement for your life that has been inspired by God?

Chapter 2
Change the Atmosphere!

"But You are holy, Enthroned in the praises of Israel"

(Psalm 22:3)

G od is enthroned in the praises of His people. Where His throne is, there is His government (authority) and power (miracles). Worship is a tool that releases a supernatural realm on earth. When we worship, God arrives and brings us into the supernatural! Worship is a gate we enter through into the presence of God. As we cross over the gates of thanksgiving we enter the courts of praise. Consider the Psalmist who declared:

Enter into His gates with thanksgiving, And into His courts with praise. Be thankful to Him, and bless His name (Psalm 100:4).

Worship is a tool that releases a supernatural realm on earth. Ministry leaders will see greater manifestations of the presence of God when they learn how to govern the moving of the Spirit. Worship puts our attention on God the Father and the Lord Jesus and not on our problems and needs. We shouldn't seek His hand unless we are seeking His face.

Just as an empty balloon has no shape or purpose until it is filled with air, praise brings form to what God is doing in our lives. Praise makes God bigger in our present situations and carries us into a place of faith.

Praise and worship create an atmosphere of power. We have authority to change the atmosphere wherever we are! A thermometer will merely tell us the temperature, but a *thermostat will change the temperature!* Christians must become thermostats that change the temperature through their praise and worship.

In the atmosphere of heaven, we receive healing, power and revelation. We must set a high priority on praise and worship when we gather so that we can operate in the realm of the supernatural. When we gather, we should expect:

- Prophecy
- Deliverance
- Preaching
- Healing
- Miracles

We Are Firstly Worshippers

Before we are intercessors, prophets, healers, or miracle workers, we are worshippers. All other ministries are the overflow. Worshipping is a practical way to experience daily the presence of God. Praise and worship is not about being healed, delivered and saved, but rather about worshipping the Healer, Deliverer and

Savior for who He is! We receive healing when we begin to come to God as Healer.

We have been given the privilege to worship the King of the Universe and His glorious Son Jesus. Many Christians will only worship when they *feel* good, or when they like the sound of the music or the song. Worship is more conducive if these elements are incorporated, but it is not dependent upon them. **Worship is an act of the will!** Worship is not just emotion; devotion must lead your emotion. Hear the words of David:

I will praise you, O LORD, with all my heart; I will tell of all your wonders. I will be glad and rejoice in you; I will sing praise to your name, O Most High. (Psalm 9:1-2)

- I will praise
- I will tell
- I will be glad
- I will sing

Hear the repetitive "I will's" in these verses. David was one who worshipped the LORD in the good times and the bad. He had the revelation that worshipping God strengthened him so that he could be empowered to accomplish God's will for his life.

But I will sing of your strength, in the morning I will sing of your love; for you are my fortress, my refuge in times of trouble. O my Strength, I sing praise to you; you, O God, are my fortress, my loving God. (Psalm 59:16-17)

- Do you have an attitude of worship?
- Do you understand the power available to you through the act worshipping?

In your body, you have over 650 skeletal muscles controlled by your brain. Some of these muscles are activated by your will, while others function without your knowledge. When was the last time you decided to digest your food, pump your blood or blink your eye? These involuntary muscles function operate like a computer, freeing our minds to focus on using our bodies as temples of worship.

I am able to lift my hands in praise, dance in His presence and shout His name because the LORD created me. He programmed my brain to manage the mundane functions so I can decide to take care of the holy functions. I was made by a loving God in order to release His love on planet earth!

Music Can Change the Atmosphere

Music has great power as a weapon to release deliverance from evil spirits. Music can cast demons out of tormented people. In ancient Israel, people understood the authority that music carried in the realm of the Spirit.

> *Now the Spirit of the LORD had departed from Saul, and an evil spirit from the LORD tormented him. Saul's attendants said to him, "See, an evil spirit from God is tormenting you. Let our lord command his servants here to search for someone who can play the harp. He will play when the evil spirit from God comes upon you, and you will feel better."*
> (1 Samuel 16:14-16)

King Saul was a demonized man. He was controlling and insecure. At times the Spirit of God moved upon him, but at other times he was murderous and vile. Those around Saul saw that he was being tormented in his soul and suggested he find a harpist.

> *So Saul said to his attendants, "Find someone who plays well and bring him to me." One of the servants answered, "I have seen a son of Jesse of Bethlehem who knows how to play the harp. He is a brave man and a warrior. He speaks well and is a fine-looking man. And the LORD is with him."* (vs. 17-18)

This is the first time Saul meets David. Though a simple shepherd boy, unnoticed by his own father amidst his seven brothers, David was a king. He first served Saul not as a warrior, but as a worshipper. Demons could not remain in his presence because he played with such skill and spiritual authority.

Whenever the spirit from God came upon Saul, David would take his harp and play. Then relief would come to Saul; he would feel better, and the evil spirit would leave him. (vs. 23)

Notice the evil spirit *left* Saul when David played the harp. Scripture does not mention him even singing. The mere authority in his fingers as he strummed the strings on his harp drove out evil! If Saul received deliverance when his walk with God was corrupt, imagine the deliverance possible for those who are righteous through the blood of Jesus!

Being a worshipper does not make you weak. I often share that revival will happen when men start dancing! Far from being weak, David was a worshipper and a warrior! Sometimes when you step out to worship God with all your might others will persecute you and mock you! David's wife despised him because he was a worshipper.

Now as the ark of the LORD came into the City of David, Michal, Saul's daughter, looked through a window and saw King David leaping and whirling before the LORD; and she despised him in her heart. (2 Samuel 6:16)

David, though a king, did not hold back his worship to the King! David knew that abandoning himself in worship would bring forth fruit in his life. Michal took offense and tried to shame him.

Then David returned to bless his household. And Michal the daughter of Saul came out to meet David, and said, "How glorious was the king of Israel today, uncovering himself today

17

> *in the eyes of the maids of his servants, as one of the base
> fellows shamelessly uncovers himself!" So David said to
> Michal, "It was before the Lord, who chose me instead of your
> father and all his house, to appoint me ruler over the people of
> the Lord, over Israel. Therefore I will play music before the
> Lord. And I will be even more undignified than this, and will
> be humble in my own sight. But as for the maidservants of
> whom you have spoken, by them I will be held in honor."
> Therefore Michal the daughter of Saul had no children to the
> day of her death.* (2 Samuel 6:20-23)

Michal despised radical worship and remained childless, demonstrating how anyone who opposes true worship will not see fruit. The supernatural realm will not be released without making yourself small and making God big!

We must understand that worship is sometimes warfare. People will bring in a judgmental and critical spirit that will try to put a wet blanket over our gathering places. Like David, we must worship with all our might to bring heaven to earth.

Releasing Authority from Heaven to Earth

Music created by God's people brings authority from heaven to earth. It releases the kingdom of God in this realm by saturating the atmosphere with songs of deliverance. When Elisha needed revelation in a difficult situation, he called for a harpist. *"'But now bring me a harpist.' While the harpist was playing, the hand of the LORD came upon Elisha"* (2 Kings 3:15). The hand of the LORD is a metaphor used in describing the power of God. When Scriptures refer to the hand of God, our mind sees five fingers and a palm, but Biblical thought sees the function of the hand, not the form.

When we need revelation in a difficult place, we should call for the musicians. Revelation will manifest itself in power and the hand of God will come upon us.

The touch of God is received from worshipping hearts; worshippers are able to give and are also more likely to receive from God. Worship brings the reality of our situations in perspective. Jesus said, *"God is Spirit, and those who worship Him must worship in spirit and truth"* (John 4:24). I like to translate the word 'truth' as *reality*. Worship brings us into reality and knowing our reality makes us free! Jesus said, *"And you shall know the truth, and the truth shall make you free"* (John 8:32).

Many people in our culture do not understand the necessity of worship. We do not worship God because He is insecure and needs our encouragement: we worship Him because a King must be worshipped. As we give Him reverence, He graces us with His Spirit. We must not come to worship to be entertained- we come to enter in! As the author of Hebrews says:

Let us then approach the throne of grace with confidence, so that we may receive mercy and find grace to help us in our time of need. (Hebrews 4:16)

With a mix of boldness and humility, we can approach His throne and surround Him with our praises.

Reflection

1. Is worship an act of emotion or an act of devotion? In what way should it be an act of devotion and in what way should it be an act of emotion?
2. When David played his harp, an evil spirit left King Saul. What is the connection between worship and deliverance?
3. What happened to Michal, the wife of David, when she was critical of her husband's undignified worship?
4. Describe how worship is a gate into God's presence.

Chapter 3
Our Passionate Duty!

Worship is our duty to the King, but it must also be our passion. Our decision to worship is made regardless of our emotional status. Once we make this conscience shift in our mindset concerning worship, there will be a tremendous outpouring of His Spirit upon our congregations. As the late Ruth Heflin said, *"We must praise Him until we can worship Him and then we must worship Him until His glory descends."* Our goal as we worship is to touch heaven and to release heaven on earth.

When all the Israelites saw the fire coming down and the glory of the LORD above the temple, they knelt on the pavement with their faces to the ground, and they worshiped and gave thanks to the LORD, saying, "He is good; his love endures forever." (2 Chronicles 7:3)

We must not neglect our duty to worship our King. When we fail, we miss out on His glory that brings us facedown before Him. As Hezekiah encouraged the priests of his day:

My sons, do not be negligent now, for the LORD has chosen you to stand before him and serve him, to minister before him and to burn incense. (2 Chronicles 29:11)

What an honor we have been given! To stand before the King of the universe and serve Him in our worship! When I first began to lead others in worship, I questioned my motives. Hezekiah's words to the priests of his day taught me a number of lessons.

1. Do not be negligent in worship!

There is a temptation in our world to bypass worship so that we can get to the Word of God to be instructed. The reality is that worship is the candle that illuminates the truth in His Word! Our worship is the fire the drives out the cold draft of the world so we are positioned to receive His instruction. We must not neglect our duty to honor our King in worship during gathering times.

For a season of my life, the enemy was accusing me of drawing attention to myself as I led worship. Satan was trying to tempt me to be less passionate before God. In this time, the LORD showed me an arrow that was pointing upward toward Him. I sensed the LORD say to me, "You are an arrow that points people to me! As you flash and shine, people begin to look up at me and not at  you. Your purpose is fulfilled as an arrow pointing to me! Do not be afraid to stand before me anymore. Do not neglect your duty to point others to me with everything that is within you!" What the LORD spoke to me that day continually allows me to lead with boldness and confidence. Don't let Satan put out your fire!

2. Worship is a service to Him.

Worship is our service to the LORD. When we worship, we serve and when we serve we worship. Worship involves our entire life and overflows into everything we do. Peter wrote to the early Christians:

But you are a chosen people, a royal priesthood, a holy nation, a people belonging to God, that you may declare the praises of him who called you out of darkness into his wonderful light.
(1 Peter 2:9)

Our duty is to declare the praises of He who called us out of darkness! When we see our worship as our duty *and* our passion, we avoid the trap of only being led by emotions. Emotions are a vital part of how we should enter His presence, but our service to Him must be driven by our commitment.

I view my duty as a worshipper in the same way a priest would view his duties in the tabernacle. These duties were part of his job description unto the LORD.

Command the Israelites to bring you clear oil of pressed olives for the light so that the lamps may be kept burning. In the Tent of Meeting, outside the curtain that is in front of the Testimony, Aaron and his sons are to keep the lamps burning before the LORD from evening till morning. (Exodus. 27:20-21)

The Levites had a responsibility to keep their lamps burning with clear oil. The oil had a fragrance, warmth and shine. Their service to the LORD was to keep the fires burning. Our worship must burn on a daily basis even though sometimes starting a fire requires much effort! Don't stop until you see the flames and feel the warmth of the fire!

3. You are chosen to stand before Him.

Out of the twelve tribes of Israel, descended from the twelve sons of Jacob, the Levitical tribe was chosen to be set apart in a special way. Jacob, married to both Leah and Rachel, favored the more beautiful Rachel, but God opened the womb of Leah while Rachel remained barren. Leah named her son Levi, meaning *"to be attached to or joined to"*, as a statement of faith in hope that she would one day be attached to her husband.

The Levites, descended from Levi, were chosen to be set apart in a special way. They rallied to Moses to deal with the sin of the golden calf (Ex. 32:26). Only they could approach the sanctuary without dying (Num. 3:10); they were the ones given wholly unto the Lord (Num. 8:16). They were in charge of the tabernacle, the tent in which God dwelt during the time between the Exodus from Egypt until the building of the temple (Num. 1:50). The care of the tabernacle was a solemn responsibility shared by the male Levites between the ages of 30 and 50.

The born-again believers, the Body of Christ, are the new Levites of the kingdom of God, chosen to stand in His dwelling place. Just as Leah desired to be attached to her husband, so should we desire to be joined with God. Like a button that keeps a coat together, worship keeps us connected with God.

4. You must burn before Him.

Hezekiah told the priests to minister before the LORD and to burn incense before Him. To smell the incense, there must first be a fire. Fire stirs up a myriad of emotions and responses! Some bring a load of wood and others bring a bucket of water.

There is a place that we can come to in our praise in worship where our hearts burn for God with a holy passion. I want to be like David who declares: *"My soul yearns, even faints, for the courts of the LORD; my heart and my flesh cry out for the living God"* (Psalm 84:2). I love those times in my life where even my physical body is yearning to be in God's presence. Nothing else can satisfy! I am physically addicted to the presence of God and nothing can keep me from his courts. When I lose the sense of his presence, I become like a fish out of water, flopping around, just to get back in the place where I find life!

One night, my wife was making spaghetti for dinner and had to give out smaller portions of the sauce. Once our boys were seated in the dining room, the call came from the kitchen,

"Whoever wants more spaghetti sauce, come and get it!" You would have thought a gun just fired in a 100-yard dash! By the time one of my sons got to the kitchen stove, he realized his plate was empty; his spaghetti had slid off the plate during his mad dash!

Whoever wants more of God, come and get Him! Hunger for more can become messy at times but we must send out the call! Psalm 23:5 says, *"My cup overflows"*. Some respond, "What a blessing," others, "What a mess!" No matter what the result, we should cherish hunger for God above all else!

Our duty to worship requires us to burn, but part of our duty is to burn the right kind of fire. We must be a *holy* fire. When we worship, it must come from a life that is grounded in a covenant relationship with God's Son, Jesus Christ. Worshippers who dishonor Jesus through disobedience put their lives at risk!

Beware of Unauthorized Fire!

Two of Aaron's sons failed to burn the right fire before the LORD. They used a fire that was *not* authorized.

Aaron's sons Nadab and Abihu took their censers, put fire in them and added incense; and they offered unauthorized fire before the LORD, contrary to his command. So fire came out from the presence of the LORD and consumed them, and they died before the LORD. (Leviticus 10:1-2)

Prior to this tragedy, the glory of the LORD was being poured out! The atmosphere was powerful and the people were facedown in awe of what God was doing.

Moses and Aaron then went into the Tent of Meeting. When they came out, they blessed the people; and the glory of the LORD appeared to all the people. Fire came out from the presence of the LORD and consumed the burnt offering and the fat portions on the altar. And when all the people saw it, they shouted for joy and fell facedown (Leviticus 9:23-24).

Unfortunately, Nadab and Abihu did not honor the LORD with their lifestyles, yet still wanted to burn incense before God. Most scholars believe they were drunk and carelessly burned the improper incense.

Yahweh commanded the burning of certain incense that released a thick smoke that would actually cover the Ark of the Covenant. The smoke that was released from the authorized incense covered the LORD so that He could remain unseen. Nadab and Abihu saw the Yahweh and died on the spot. The altar of incense is described in Exodus 30:

Put the altar in front of the curtain that shields the ark of the covenant law—before the atonement cover that is over the tablets of the covenant law—where I will meet with you. Aaron must burn fragrant incense on the altar every morning when he tends the lamps. He must burn incense again when he lights the lamps at twilight so incense will burn regularly before the Lord for the generations to come. Do not offer on this altar any other incense or any burnt offering or grain offering, and do not pour a drink offering on it. (Exodus 30:6-9)

The altar of incense in Exodus 30 is a type of worship. Prayers are heard but praises are smelled. The smoke from this altar was to be burned while Aaron lit the lamps in the tabernacle signifying that we must worship while we do the work of the LORD.

The altar of incense was set apart for fragrance only! No other sacrifice could be made on this altar. We cannot mix our worship with guilt offerings or sin offerings. Our worship is to be set apart for Him, pure and holy. The LORD commanded Moses to place a fragrance at the entrance of the tabernacle. God desires that His place of worship is inviting to all our senses, even smell!!

Make a fragrant blend of incense, the work of a perfumer. It is to be salted and pure and sacred. Grind some of it to powder and place it in front of the ark of the covenant law in the tent of meeting, where I will meet with you. It shall be most holy to you. Do not make any incense with this formula for yourselves; consider it holy to the LORD. (Exodus 30:35-37)

The incense of worship was created to make fragrant His presence. God warns His children not to use this fragrance upon themselves! All worship teams and leaders take heed!

Worship is about honor. The Hebrew word for honor is *kabed* which means, *"to be heavy with goods, property, money"*.[3] To survive in God's presence, our fire must release a heavy smoke, which flows out of a lifestyle of humility, honor and holiness. The prophet Isaiah had an encounter with God and it ruined him!

I saw the Lord, high and exalted, seated on a throne; and the train of his robe filled the temple. Above him were seraphim, each with six wings: With two wings they covered their faces, with two they covered their feet, and with two they were flying. And they were calling to one another: "Holy, holy, holy is the Lord Almighty; the whole earth is full of his glory." At the sound of their voices the doorposts and thresholds shook and the temple was filled with smoke. (Isaiah 6:1-4)

Isaiah tells that at the sound of their voices the temple was filled with smoke. Here we discover a principle about God's presence that our lives must burn with glory as we worship Him. Only a holy fire will release the thick smoke that will cover His glorious presence. To stand before the LORD and minister requires a certain lifestyle both on and off the stage. I chose to live a life that is authorized of the LORD so that I can burn before Him and live.

---

[3] Zodhiates, Spiros, and John R. Kohlenberger. *The Hebrew-Greek Key Study Bible: New International Version.* Chattanooga, TN: AMG Pub., 1996. 1522

For we are to God the aroma of Christ among those who are being saved and those who are perishing. To the one we are the smell of death; to the other, the fragrance of life.
(2 Corinthians 2:15)

Every time we come to worship we must make the choice to release the fragrance of His praise or to hold on to it and waste it! The only way to release the aroma of a perfume is to open the bottle. One of the greatest act of worship is described in Luke 7:37-38:

When a woman who had lived a sinful life in that town learned that Jesus was eating at the Pharisee's house, she brought an alabaster jar of perfume, and as she stood behind him at his feet weeping, she began to wet his feet with her tears. She wiped them with her hair, kissed them and poured perfume on them.

Mark 14:3 says, " *...she broke the jar and poured the perfume on his head."* Jesus spoke of her saying, *"I tell you the truth, wherever the gospel is preached throughout the world, what she has done will also be told, in memory of her"* (Mark 14:9). If only Christ could say that of us! What are we missing in our worship that keeps us from receiving such praise from Christ?

Ecclesiastes 10:1 says, *"...dead flies give perfume a bad smell."* Ungodly attitudes and behaviors are 'dead flies' that cause our worship to become an unpleasant odor instead of a beautiful fragrance. Pride, envy and lust must be plucked out of our sacred anointing oil. The longer these "dead flies" remain the less potent our praise!

The LORD commanded Moses to use fragrant anointing oil throughout the tabernacle where God would dwell.

Make these into a sacred anointing oil, a fragrant blend, the work of a perfumer. It will be the sacred anointing oil. Then use it to anoint the Tent of Meeting (and everything in it)...You shall consecrate them so they will be most holy, and whatever touches them will be holy (Ex 30:25-29 *italics mine*).

Fragrant praise consecrates an atmosphere so that God can come and inhabit His sanctuary. Scoop the dead flies out of your anointing and break open the jar of your fragrance. Wipe His feet with your hair and kiss His feet. Pour yourself out for the One who loves you so passionately!

Moses then said to Aaron, "This is what the LORD spoke of when he said: "'Among those who approach me I will show myself holy; in the sight of all the people I will be honored.'"
(Leviticus 10:1-3)

Throughout the Bible, you can read about different people who failed to honor God in their lifestyle while engaging in their duty of worship. When we approach the LORD, we must not take lightly our responsibility. Asher Intrater said:

In Hebrew the root word for worship, U-B-D, means both work and worship. Work and worship are parallel thoughts. Worship implies both spiritual adoration and submission to authority.[4]

We are not truly worshipping unless our lives are submitted to the authority of God's Son, Jesus Christ. Passionate adoration void of submission to Christ cannot ever be considered worship. Electricity flows properly through a system of wires. One wire is the power wire and the other is the ground wire. Both must be connected to have useful power flowing. If you disconnect one wire, you will have no power. If you disconnect the other; the ground wire, you will have power, but you could be electrocuted!

---

[4] Intrater, Asher (2011-11-16). Who Ate Lunch with Abraham (Kindle Locations 1961-1964).

In our worship, our ground wire is our submission to the authority of Jesus in our lives. Power flows safely into our lives and into the lives of others when we worship with grounded lives! Worship brings great power, but with it comes great responsibility!

King David's Worship Blunder

David made the mistake of not following God's set instructions in how he was to worship. His lack of obedience ended in a disaster that took the life of one his leaders.

David again brought together out of Israel chosen men, thirty thousand in all...They set the ark of God on a new cart and brought it from the house of Abinadab, which was on the hill... David and the whole house of Israel were celebrating with all their might before the LORD, with songs and with harps, lyres, tambourines, sistrums and cymbals...
(2 Samuel 6:1-5)

Imagine 30,000 people gathering with their instruments to celebrate with all their might in your town! This was no small gathering!

The ark of God represented the presence of God. David was attempting to bring the ark to Jerusalem where it belonged. Good intentions do not always bring good results. The LORD said through the prophet Hosea, **"my people are destroyed from lack of knowledge"** (Hosea 4:6). What did David miss that brought death to one of his worship leaders?

Common Mistakes Made in Worship

1. We follow the way of the world

David instructed that the ark be carried on a new cart. He probably got this idea from the Philistines who **"...placed the ark of the LORD on the cart"** (1 Samuel 6:11). David made the mistake of looking to the world instead of looking to the Word. How we carry the presence of God in our life will determine whether we live or die!   David later discovered the way God wanted him to have the ark carried.

So the priests and Levites consecrated themselves in order to bring up the ark of the LORD, the God of Israel. And the Levites carried the ark of God with the poles on their shoulders, as Moses had commanded in accordance with the word of the LORD. (1 Chronicles 15:13-15)

Yahweh commanded certain people to carry the ark and that they carry it on poles, not carts! Placing the ark on a cart put it in danger of falling. The Levites were told to carry it on their shoulders and not pull it by oxen. David's failure to follow these instructions put those around the ark in a dangerous position!

2) We try to control what God is doing

Uzzah was one of the leaders helping bring the Ark of the Covenant back to Jerusalem.   The event must have been spectacular as they journeyed to bring this symbol of God's presence into the Holy City. But things did not go as planned!

When they came to the threshing floor of Nacon, Uzzah reached out and took hold of the ark of God, because the oxen stumbled. The LORD's anger burned against Uzzah because of his irreverent act; therefore God struck him down and he died there beside the ark of God... (2 Samuel 6:6-7)

Imagine having to take the microphone at this point and tell the 30,000 folks what happened! "Ladies and gentlemen! Thanks for coming out to see the ark! Well, we aren't going to Jerusalem today! God just killed our worship leader! Have a nice day!" Most people, including myself, never understood how Uzzah could have been struck down when he was trying to save the ark from falling. However, when we don't follow in the set patterns God has set in place on earth, we often have to take control. Uzzah's response to take control was due to an improper pattern of ministry. David's casual approach to worship brought death to his plans and forced him to reconsider his approach based on God's Word and not on the world's ways.

Then David was angry because the LORD's wrath had broken out against Uzzah, ...David was afraid of the LORD that day and said, "How can the ark of the LORD ever come to me?"
(2 Samuel 6:8-9)

After this event, David had the fear of the LORD. The fear of the LORD is actually a gift of the Spirit. The prophet Isaiah referred to these gifts in the coming Messiah:

The Spirit of the Lord will rest on him— the Spirit of wisdom and of understanding, the Spirit of counsel and of power, the Spirit of knowledge and of the fear of the Lord— and he will delight in the fear of the Lord. He will not judge by what he sees with his eyes, or decide by what he hears with his ears.
(Isaiah 11:2-3)

The seven gifts of the Spirit here in Isaiah can be represented as one branch of the menorah, a seven-branched candelabra used in the temple. The central branch of the menorah is the fear of the LORD in which we must delight. As we light each branch of the menorah we shine brighter in this dark world and have the ability to discern good from evil.

The fear of the LORD is not as much a fear of approaching God as it is a deep allegiance to the teachings of Scripture. *Casual Christianity causes casualties!* We must not be careless in our understanding that God means what He says. The influences around us will pressure us, even in the little things, to disregard God's Word. My prayer is that I walk in the fear of the LORD all the days of my life!

3) We take publicly what hasn't happened privately

One of the greatest dangers is to mistake performance for worship. The world loves a good performance, but if the heavens remain closed, we must pull the plug. Worship should be done with excellence in skill and with excellence in spirit. The only way to develop excellence in spirit is to have private time with Jesus.

One morning I went into prayer and I was overwhelmed with a sense of inadequacy before the LORD. Then I heard the LORD speak to me, saying, *"As you worship my Son Jesus, you become more like Him. Feeling guilty will not change you, but worshipping my Son will transform you into His image."* At that point, I took the focus off myself and placed it upon Jesus. I felt the heavens opened and my spirit revived!

We must develop a deep relationship with the LORD in private before we can have a platform in public. Deep roots are needed for tall trees. The taller the tree, the deeper the roots must grow, lest a single storm brings the entire tree crashing down!

Foundations are constructed before the building can be built. When a new project is being built, there is usually an architectural rendering that shows us what the building will look like when it is completed. For the much of the project, the only thing you can see is a big hole, with lots of mud and dirt.

Our lives are much like a building project. People are eager to see the finished project but we feel like a big hole in the ground with piles of dirt spread out. We must not take the building of the foundations for our lives lightly! We must be grounded, deeply rooted in Christ. Having a daily personal worship service must become a priority so that you will be able to stand for Him in public.

After Uzzah's death, David reconsidered how to carry the ark of the LORD into Jerusalem. Because he was afraid, David left the ark at the house of Obed-Edom.

He was not willing to take the ark of the LORD to be with him in the City of David. Instead, he took it aside to the house of Obed-Edom the Gittite. (2 Samuel 6:10)

During this time, something began to happen in the house of Obed-Edom.

Now King David was told, "The LORD has blessed the household of Obed-Edom and everything he has, because of the ark of God." (vs. 6:12)

I believe the LORD is showing us that He must be lifted up first in our homes before He can be lifted up effectively in our city! As Obed-Edom worshipped before the ark in his house, everything he had was blessed! When you have the presence of God in your home, your family, your work, your finances, your appliances- everything you have will be blessed. The blessing of God upon Obed-Edom's house brought David to action.

So David went down and brought up the ark of God from the house of Obed-Edom to the City of David with rejoicing. David, wearing a linen ephod, danced before the LORD with all his might, while he and the entire house of Israel brought

34

up the ark of the LORD with shouts and the sound of trumpets. (2 Samuel 6:12-15)

This time, David followed the LORD's instruction on how to carry the ark. God had to do a work in David's heart before He could successfully bring the ark into Jerusalem. He acquired the fear of the LORD, which is the beginning or foundation of wisdom.

Reflection

1. Fill in the blanks: *"We must _____ Him until we can _____ Him and then we must _____ Him until His _____ descends."*
2. Is it O.K. to be exuberant in our worship of God and His Son Jesus Christ? Use the analogy of an arrow when giving your answer.
3. Why did Uzzah die when he tried to keep the Ark of the Covenant from falling?
4. Describe how worship must be more than just passionate adoration. Are you grounded in God's Word so that you can also be empowered by God's Spirit?

Chapter 4
Zeal for Worship

Satan deeply opposes any worshipper because he fears the manifest presence of God. I love to quote Psalm 46:1: *"God is our refuge and strength, a very present help in trouble."* This verse does not say God is just present, but *very present!* In certain places I feel His presence, but in other places I feel God is very present. I believe the difference between present and very present can be achieved through our zeal for Him. Powerful, passionate worship brings tremendous blessing to our gatherings, but tremendous resistance can also follow in the spiritual realm because we are making offerings with fire! The reality is Satan opposes us because He is jealous of our position in worship!

Lucifer: The Angel of Worship

Most scholars believe Lucifer (personal name of Satan) was the angel in charge of worship before he rebelled.

You were anointed as a guardian cherub, for so I ordained you. You were on the holy mount of God; you walked among the fiery stones. (Ezekiel 28:14)

Three angels are mentioned in Scripture by name. Gabriel was the messenger angel and is found in action in the book of Daniel and in the gospel of Luke coming to Mary, the mother of Jesus.

The angel answered, "I am Gabriel. I stand in the presence of God, and I have been sent to speak to you and to tell you this good news. (Luke 1:19)

Gabriel delivered the message of the LORD in the same manner we receive mail. He was given the word of the LORD and delivers the package to whom it is sent. In book of Daniel, the angel Gabriel was resisted by a demonic entity called the Prince of the Persian kingdom.

Then he continued, "Do not be afraid, Daniel. Since the first day that you set your mind to gain understanding and to humble yourself before your God, your words were heard, and I have come in response to them. But the prince of the Persian kingdom resisted me twenty-one days" (Daniel 10:13-14).

The angel Gabriel was detained for twenty-one days because a demonic entity prevented him from giving Daniel his message from the LORD. Another angel, Michael, the warrior angel was sent to help.

Then Michael, one of the chief princes, came to help me, because I was detained there with the king of Persia. Now I

have come to explain to you what will happen to your people in
the future, for the vision concerns a time yet to come.
(Daniel 10:13-14)

Michael's job description was to be a militant warrior. He and his team of angels fought against Lucifer.

And there was war in heaven. Michael and his angels fought against the dragon, and the dragon and his angels fought back. But he was not strong enough, and they lost their place in heaven. The great dragon was hurled down—that ancient serpent called the devil, or Satan, who leads the whole world astray. He was hurled to the earth, and his angels with him.
(Revelation 12:7-11)

After Satan's fall, I imagine the job posting in heaven said something like this:

JOB OPENING IN HEAVEN

Persons needed to fill the current void of worship that covers the throne. Responsibilities include continual praise and worship done in Spirit and in truth. Must be radically committed, loyal, and set apart from the world. Humility and passion for God the Father and His Son Jesus are necessary. The recently vacated position will now be filled by not just

39

one person, but instead a team of loud, willing laborers from Earth who have been purchased for God by the blood of Jesus. No previous experience necessary. Position to be filled immediately.

In the same manner that Gabriel was the messenger angel and Michael the warrior angel with specific duties to perform, Lucifer was created to worship before the throne of God. Most scholars believe that Lucifer was a guardian cherub (Ez. 28:14) covering the throne of God in praise. He lost his position because of pride and rebellion, but now you and I can worship in humility and holiness. The church is called to fill the void of His praise!

I believe the following scriptures, applied to the king of Tyre, paint a picture of Lucifer before he was kicked out of heaven.

You were in Eden, the garden of God. Every precious stone was your covering. The sardius, topaz, and diamond, Beryl, onyx, and jasper, Sapphire, turquoise, and emerald with gold. The workmanship of your timbrels and pipes was prepared for you on the day you were created. "You were the anointed cherub who covers; I established you; You were on the holy mountain of God; You walked back and forth in the midst of fiery stones. You were perfect in your ways from the day you were created, till iniquity was found in you. (Ezekiel 28:12-15)

Lucifer is depicted in this passage as an angel with percussion and wind instruments flowing out of his being. Precious stones covered him that resonated different tones and frequencies as the sound vibrations flowed through them.

40

Another picture of Lucifer comes from the book of Isaiah that describes *"the noise of your harps"* (Isaiah 14:11).

I find it hard to believe that Lucifer could have had this position! The realization of Lucifer's original purpose reminds me that leadership in worship must be accompanied by the fear of the LORD. Lucifer had all the skill and talent that creation could offer, given to lift up praises before God. Instead, Lucifer took pride in himself and rebelled. Yahweh speaks to him saying, *"In the pride of your heart you say, "I am a god""*. (Ezekiel 28:2). Pride led to his down fall.

> *So I drove you in disgrace from the mount of God, and I expelled you, O guardian cherub, from among the fiery stones. Your heart became proud on account of your beauty, and you corrupted your wisdom because of your splendor. So I threw you to the earth;* (Ezekiel 28:16-17)

Many of our false idols in society are musicians with big egos and foul lifestyles. God is calling a unique group of people to worship before his throne.

Join the Eunuch Club

What is so unique about eunuchs? Traditionally, eunuchs were castrated males who were put in charge over the care of the royal women in a king's palace. They were renowned for their faithfulness to their masters.

In Acts 8:27 Philip the evangelist *"...met an Ethiopian eunuch, an important official in charge of all the treasury of Candace, queen of the Ethiopians."* In many ancient cultures you could not be in the king's presence unless you were castrated! A eunuch was a trusted position that required intense devotion to the very core of your being.

Daniel was brought into the service of the king of Babylon, leading many scholars believe Daniel was made a eunuch because he served the *"prince of the eunuchs"* (Daniel 1:7 KJV). Kings

41

could trust eunuchs because they lacked the ability to have descendants who could sit on the future throne, allowing a king to be more at peace in the knowledge his servants held no rebellious aspirations.

Eunuchs and worshipers alike must not be ambitious or self-seeking. We must serve recognizing there is only One who deserves to sit on the throne of His Father; His name is Jesus. We are allowed to sit on the throne, but only on His lap!

In the book of Esther, we read that Esther *"...was placed under the care of Hegai, the king's eunuch..."* (Esther 2:3). His job was to guard the beautiful women of the harem as they prepared themselves with beauty treatments to meet the King.

As a leader of worship, I must become a eunuch in service to my King. Worship leaders must cut off even their ability to desire what rightfully belongs to the King. I long for the day when my master can fully trust me with His bride as I prepare her for His coming.

As Esther went to present herself before the King, *"...she asked for nothing other than what Hegai, the king's eunuch, who was in charge of the harem, suggested."* (v.15). Because Esther heeded the advice of Hegai, as she went before the King *"...she won his approval more than any of the other virgins... and [he] made her queen..."* (v.17).

Worshipers must understand protocol. Protocol is defined as *"a code of correct conduct that governs the affairs of how one ought to act in the presence of royalty."*[5] As we worship we are entering into the presence of the King of the Universe! Protocol will determine whether or not our sacrifices will be accepted. As we are reminded in Leviticus 19:5, *"sacrifice it in such a way that it will be accepted on your behalf."*

As the Ethiopian eunuch was in charge of a great treasury, so is each of us. Yet we must not violate the trust we have been given by God and take glory for ourselves as we worship. The

---

[5] Ehrlich, Eugene. Oxford American Dictionary. New York: Oxford UP, 1980.

decision to become selfless in our own passions is what makes for spiritual eunuch of worship. The cost is great, but so is the reward.

For this is what the LORD says; 'To the eunuchs who keep my Sabbaths, who choose what pleases me and hold fast to my covenant— to them I will give within my temple and its walls a memorial and a name better than sons and daughters; I will give an everlasting name that will not be cut off (Isaiah 56:4-5).

The LORD is seeking worshippers passionless toward their own lust, yet passionate to make the bride beautiful for her King. Eunuchs have decided to put those lusts to death in themselves in order to bring beauty to the King's bride.

The Power of Loyalty

Loyalty is defined as "affectionate allegiance" and is the precursor to the fire of zeal. Like dry wood and chaff, loyalty creates the atmosphere for the fire to spark. God's strength follows those who are loyal. *"For the eyes of the Lord range throughout the earth to strengthen those whose hearts are fully committed to him."* (2 Chronicles 16:9)

Loyalty is more than following the command of another. Loyalty infers a heart of love, respect and honor toward the one you are following. In his book Exploring Worship, Bob Sorge wrote, "Loyalty is esteemed as a commodity of great worth, which God is always seeking."[6] Loyalty is a character quality that attracts supernatural power needed to move mountains in our lives.

God is searching for loyal people. When God is on the Internet, He types in l-o-y-a-l-t-y into His search engine and presses enter. When He finds a loyal person, He strengthens them in what they are doing. Christians are empowered through their affectionate allegiance to the LORD.

Jesus was devoted to His Father in heaven and His loyalty was contagious. Jesus never had to sit his disciples down and force

---

[6] Sorge, Bob. *Exploring Worship: A Practical Guide to Praise and Worship.* Canandaigua, NY: Sorge, 1987. Print.

them to learn how to pray. His disciples saw Him enjoying time with His Heavenly Father and saw the results of His ministry and wanted what Jesus had! His loyal devotion to pray was fueled by His passion for the Father.

When Jesus' disciples sought to be taught on prayer, He said to them, *"When you pray, say: 'Father, hallowed be your name, your kingdom come'"* (Luke 11:2). For the kingdom of God to advance on the earth, we must 'hallow' God's name. John Piper defines the word hallow as follows:

To hallow God's name means to put it in a class by itself and to cherish and honor it above every claim to our allegiance .[7]

When we approach the Father, our worship must be in loyal, affectionate devotion that is uncompromised and incomparable to any other thing in existence. Our affectionate allegiance is the way we hallow His name.

God is a Jealous God

The Scriptures declare to us that Yahweh is a jealous God and in our worship we must not forget what is written: *"Do not worship any other god, for the LORD, whose name is Jealous, is a jealous God"* (Exodus 34:14).

Jealousy is one of the most embarrassing emotions of which to be accused. In our society an accusation of jealousy usually points to someone who is insecure, vulnerable and desperate. Yet in the Scriptures we find God Himself, whose name is Yahweh, declaring, "I am a Jealous God!"

The emotion of jealousy and anger are interconnected. Jealousy is probably one of the strongest emotions one can ever experience. King Solomon describes *"...love as strong as death, its jealousy unyielding as the grave. It burns like blazing fire, like a mighty flame"* (Song of Songs 8:6).

---

[7] Piper, John. Let the Nations Be Glad!: The Supremacy of God in Missions. Grand Rapids, MI: Baker, 1993. Print. P.35

Jealousy is a covenantal emotion. It is normal and right to be consumed with jealousy for those with whom you are in covenant. Covenant relationships are meant to be experienced in our families, in the church, and especially in our relationship with God the Father and the Lord Jesus! God is pursuing us with zeal and He is jealous for our pure devotion!

Zeal in Worship

Zeal means infers *a burning or to be hot*. It denotes fire. God Himself accomplishes His purposes through zeal and He desires us to do the same. The prophet Isaiah declares, *"The zeal of the LORD Almighty will accomplish this"* (Isaiah 9:7).

The Hebrew word for zeal, *qana*, *"...represents the act of the advancement of God and His glory over all substitutes."*[8] The word for jealous in the Hebrew language is closely connected the word for zeal. The LORD (Yahweh) permits no rivals and neither should we!

Zeal is like an unction or supernatural boost given to us through His word. We understand our call to lift up Jesus above all else. God's Word to us is an appeal for zeal to function in unction!

Zeal is not an option! We must renew our passion for the things of God on a daily basis. Zeal will be the catalyst for a fruitful life. But keep in mind that *"...it is not good to have zeal without knowledge nor to be hasty and miss the way"* (Proverbs19:2). Paul instructs the Galatians, *"It is fine to be zealous, provided the purpose is good, and to be so always and not just when I am with you"* (Galatians 4:18). We must be grounded in His Word and empowered by His Spirit. We want to be electrified not electrocuted! In our zeal for God, we must not overlook our own need for character development from brokenness.

---

[8] Zodhiates, Spiros, and John R. Kohlenberger. *The Hebrew-Greek Key Study Bible: New International Version*. Chattanooga, TN: AMG Pub., 1996. 1548

Zeal is only real when it carries over into our daily life. We must be lovers of God and a passionate bride of Christ both in public and in private. Many in church leadership are afraid to encourage zealous worship because it might give the appearance of seduction or fanaticism. But we must remember how David danced before the LORD with all his might.

David, wearing a linen ephod, danced before the LORD with all his might, while he and the entire house of Israel brought up the ark of the LORD with shouts and the sound of trumpets. (1 Samuel 6:14-15)

King David was never corrected by the LORD for dancing in his linen ephod with all His might. In fact, his humility to strip down and his zeal to dance brought glory to Yahweh His God!

Though it is not good to have zeal without knowledge, it is even worse to have knowledge without zeal! As one preacher said, *"It is easier to restrain a fanatic than it is to raise the dead!"*

Jehoash, a king of Israel was not fully delivered from his enemies because he failed to strike the arrows to the ground with unction. (2 Kings 13:14-20). Because of his lack of zeal he only received a shallow victory over his enemies. Let the worshipping church learn this lesson as well.

Crying Out Brings Deliverance

There must be a high level of zeal and exuberance in our praises if we are expecting God to respond. The Hebrew word for *cry out* is *za'ag,* which means, *"to shriek from anguish or a sense of danger"* and symbolizes *"...a crying out to God from a disturbed heart, summoning help and deliverance."* [9]

I can remember times in my life when I felt such oppression and distress that my only choice was to cry out from the depths of soul. David said, *"In my distress I called to the*

---

[9] Zodhiates, Spiros, and John R. Kohlenberger. *The Hebrew-Greek Key Study Bible: New International Version.* Chattanooga, TN: AMG Pub., 1996. 1513

46

LORD; I cried to my God for help. From His temple he heard my voice" (Psalm 18:6).

In our intellectual society, it might seem improper to do such a thing. But I must ask, do you want civil acceptance or spiritual freedom?

Reading through the book of Judges, you will discover a pattern that is repeated over and over in the life of the Israelites. Below is a diagram that describes this cycle of oppression to deliverance as we cry out to God to raise up a deliverer.

Scripture says, *"...they groaned under those who oppressed and afflicted them"* (Judges 2:18). *"But when they cried out to the LORD, He raised up a deliverer..."* (Judges 3:9). If you are facing oppression due to sickness, finances, stress or whatever is against you– cry out! He has already raised our Deliverer, and His name is Jesus!

And if the Spirit of him who raised Jesus from the dead is living in you, he who raised Christ from the dead will also give life to your mortal bodies through his Spirit, who lives in you.
(Romans 8:11)

We should maintain high expectations in our worship. As we cry out to God, supernatural happenings will become the norm! For the kingdom of God to advance, followers of Jesus must embrace zeal in their worship. Great spiritual force resides in simple physical acts of worship. The passion of God in burning in one soul will produce more fruit in eternity than a thousand pondering theologians. God is not impressed by intellect but by faith. Step out in your worship become a fool on fire for Jesus!

No Smoking in Church

I am not addressing tobacco usage at this time, but rather your spiritual condition! Christians need to stop smoking and get on fire! Smoke is a product of fire but not its replacement. Jesus wants to immerse us in the Spirit and fire. John spoke of Jesus saying, *"He will baptize you with the Holy Spirit and with fire"* (Matthew 3:11).

What does it mean to be on fire? I believe it signifies a condition of your heart whenever you come into the presence of Jesus. Is your heart longing for Him? When you prepare to come into His presence, are you trying to justify yourself, weighing out the good and bad you have done, hoping to find His approval? Or does your heart rejoice when you feel His presence, not looking to justify yourself but only to love Him with everything that is in you?

Smoke, without fire, is usually irritating, annoying, and causes everything to stink. It is caused by smoldering coals unable to come into a blaze due to moisture. I believe Ezekiel saw Jesus in a vision and this is how he described Him:

I looked, and I saw a figure like that of a man. From what appeared to be his waist down he was like fire, and from there up his appearance was as bright as glowing metal. (Ezekiel 8:2)

Jesus is on fire and when we are with Him, He causes us to burn. Paul wrote: *"For this reason I remind you to fan into flame the gift of God, which is in you through the laying on of my hands"* (2 Timothy 1:6). Take the smoldering coals in your life that you have and fan them into a flame through your worship. As we worship, every other spirit that attempts to smother your fire will be driven away! The ability to burn is inside of you. The destiny to burn is what fuels you.

48

Fire is a gift from God. The author of Hebrews writes that *"God is a consuming fire"* (Hebrews 12:29). To be full of God is to be full of fire! You cannot have the baptism of the Spirit without the baptism of fire. People do not want to see smoke, but they will run to a fire! John Wesley said, *"I set myself on fire and people come to watch me burn!"*

God reveals Himself when we gather in His name and worship Him and His Son Jesus. As we worship we can feel His Spirit and this immersion of the Spirit brings the fire of God. Every Christian should be highly flammable, and those around should be cautioned that we are at risk to burst into flames at any moment.

Reflection

1. To hallow God's name means to put it in a class by itself and to cherish and honor it above every claim to our allegiance. What are we declaring when we pray, "Father, hallowed by your name"?
2. Define what it means to be a "spiritual eunuch."
3. Why do we need a baptism of the Holy Spirit and of fire?
4. Satan lost his position in heaven. What kind of emotions does Satan have toward us because we have taken his place as worshippers around the throne of God?
5. Zeal can be defined as *"...representing the act of the advancement of God and His glory over all substitutes."* Do you apply zeal your worship?

Chapter 5

Prophetic Worship

Creative people (or artisans) have a depth in their soul that allows them to think outside of the box. They communicate through what they create, and what they create is a product of what they feel in their heart of hearts. Artists are rarely shallow people. They have a God given depth that, if not channeled and released properly, can lead to depression, drugs, addictions and even suicide. Is it any wonder why so many artistic icons end up dying at a young age?

The church must wake up to the talent she has been given through her artisans (i.e. musicians, poets, script writers, actors, graphic designers, etc.). Understanding the artistic gifting is of key importance to this generation. Souls are at stake when the church allows her creative people to lay dormant!

Nebuchadnezzar, King of Babylon, invaded Jerusalem and exiled the influential inhabitants of the city. The Babylonians developed this strategy to weaken the effectiveness of the city and to keep its inhabitants from rebelling against the foreign power. Under Babylonian rule, Jerusalem was not the same:

> *...the court officials and the leaders... the craftsmen and the artisans had gone into exile from Jerusalem... to Babylon.*
> (Jeremiah 29:2)

Satan uses the same strategy. He has stripped us of our craftsman and artisans, leaving the church weak and ineffective to impact the culture! The church needs to call creativity back into her walls.

Fully Expressing Our Emotions

Expressing emotions is often considered to be a weakness in many western societies. We often embrace the intellectual side of Christianity, yet fail to applaud the passionate, emotional side. Enthusiasm encompasses the Greek word *theo,* which means God. Those who are enthusiastic are actually *in theo*, or in God! Jesus showed us by His own life how important it is to express our emotions. Jesus wept and expressed joy and righteous anger.

Yahweh commanded the Israelites to celebrate. We should celebrate just like we should follow the Ten Commandments. *"Celebrate ...as I commanded you"* (Exodus 23:16). Celebration empowers us to live a holy life. Dancing before the LORD is a great stress reliever. Celebration connects me to others in a community because we experience the bliss of God in those moments. During our gathering times, I will often encourage the circle dance because it is a victory dance and releases unity in the body of Christ.

Many of the most sincere followers of Jesus have a hard time with joy and celebration in the house of God. We are OK with people weeping, but laughter is from the devil! Yahweh instructed the people to stop weeping, get something sweet to eat and cheer up!

Scriptures Come Alive When Celebrating

Revelation often begins with information that penetrates the heart and turns into conviction which then produces action. Celebrating takes truth and incorporates truth into our lives, especially into our children. Celebration must not be forsaken or taken lightly! We should joyfully take every opportunity to remember the goodness of God. When Jesus walked this earth, the response of the people is noted in the book of Luke:

And overwhelming astonishment and ecstasy seized them all, and they recognized and praised and thanked God; and they were filled with and controlled by reverential fear and kept saying, We have seen wonderful and strange and incredible and unthinkable things today! (Luke 5:26 Douay-Rheims Bible)

Truth must be presented in the context of celebration. In western societies, we have emphasized teaching while de-emphasizing emotion. However, truth is attached to our lives when it is planted in the soil of celebration.

Many researchers divide the brain as having a right side and a left side. The left side is the area of the brain that focuses on logic, facts, math and reason. The right side is the area of the brain that focuses on creativity, music, art and imagination. Some cultures emphasize the left side of the brain as being most useful and do not encourage right brain activities.

Our school system often devalues those children who are dominantly right brained. These children would rather write their own story instead of reading someone else's. Instead of coloring the picture, they want to create their own. They daydream and use their imagination instead of repeating facts committed to memory. Such children are sent home with a disciplinary note and scolded for not fitting into the classroom and may even be deemed a rebel.

Yet our goal should be to celebrate God's truth in creative ways. We should encourage the entire brain of every individual and be sure we are not being overly influenced by our left-brain dominant societies! The need for music, art and celebration brings the facts of the Scriptures from head knowledge to heart knowledge. We then experience the Scriptures! Our children will not only know about Jesus but they know Jesus. The realities that Jesus came to teach will be experienced as we celebrate.

God's First Act: He Created

The very first verb in the Bible is the word *bara*, which means "to create." *"In the beginning, God created..."* and every beginning must be followed by creativity and creative people. Creative people are often very spiritually attuned people. Spirituality and creativity create an atmosphere for worship to reach new heights.

> *Then the LORD said to Moses, "See, I have chosen Bezalel son of Uri, the son of Hur, of the tribe of Judah, and I have filled him with the Spirit of God, with skill, ability and knowledge in all kinds of crafts-- to make artistic designs for work in gold, silver and bronze, to cut and set stones, to work in wood, and to engage in all kinds of craftsmanship.*
> (Exodus 31:1-5)

The name *Bezalel* in Hebrew means, *"in the shadow of God."* The shadow is a place of darkness, uncertainty and even fear. Many creative people are overcome by depression and suicide because they fail to see their darkness as standing in God's shadow. Creative fires must burn in this place of darkness or the person may fall into demonic places.

Most worship leaders have increased sensitivity that allows them to sense what the Spirit of God is doing in a place. Their ability to be sensitive is a great asset to the body of Christ. However, increased sensitivity may also produce communication issues and relational problems common to many involved in

54

leading worship.

Worship, Prophets and Transformation

In Biblical times, schools of prophets would gather to prophesy and worship. One day, the prophet Samuel told Saul, the soon-to-be king of Israel, what was about to take place.

As you approach the town, you will meet a procession of prophets coming down from the high place with lyres, tambourines, flutes and harps being played before them, and they will be prophesying. The Spirit of the LORD will come upon you in power, and you will prophesy with them; and you will be changed into a different person (1 Samuel 10:5-6).

As Saul came in the midst of prophetic music, three things happened:

1. **The Spirit came upon him with power.**
2. **He began to prophesy.**
3. **He became a different person.**

This portion of scripture inspires me to expect awesome happenings in the midst of worship. When I go to get a haircut, I expect to walk out looking different; when I go into worship, I expect to walk out a different person. I no longer just sing the words of a song, but instead, I prophetically declare the future over those within the sound of my voice.

My goal as a worshipper is to visibly witness a transformation over people as I worship Jesus. A notable change happened in my spirit when I began to see myself calling forth change in lives as I ministered and recognized the power of His word. Isaiah declared the words of the LORD:

So is my word that goes out from my mouth: It will not return to me empty, but will accomplish what I desire and achieve the purpose for which I sent it (Isaiah 55:11).

To experience supernatural power in worship, we must see our worship as prayers that release heaven over us. These prayers are not just spoken— they are sung. St. Augustine taught, *"He who sings prays twice!"* Something beyond words is released into the atmosphere as we worship.

In ancient times, a king would rule his kingdom by issuing his will to his scribes who would then write the king's wishes down and pass them on to different heralds. These heralds would travel throughout the kingdom and proclaim the king's will to all areas of the kingdom. The moment the herald proclaimed the king's will from the scroll, the king's words became the law in that realm in which it was proclaimed.

Worshippers are heralds of the kingdom of God decalring the will of heaven here on earth. The King's Word becomes reality once it is proclaimed! Heaven is released on earth as we declare the praises of the One who called us out of darkness. We must not be silent anymore. Let worship arise in the hearts of His people!

Songs need to be written not about where we are, but where we **will** be. Prophecy pulls the future into the now. Write songs that are prophetic declarations of our glorious inheritance in Christ that we will soon experience.

I used to struggle with leading songs over a congregation that declared something that was not actually happening. I would sing, "Everybody's dancing!" Truth be told, no one was dancing. I would sing, "Lord, I give my all to you!" Truth be told, only a handful were even partially engaged in worship at the time. Was I wrong to sing songs that were untrue in the present? Leonard Ravenhill said, "Christians do not tell lies, they just sing them every Sunday."

As a worship leader, the good things you declare will bring the future into a present reality. You are not being untruthful, but instead are declaring a reality not yet seen. You must lead the congregation in songs of faith and hope.

Prophesying Life in a Graveyard

Worship brings life to an atmosphere and drives out darkness. The enemy understands the power of worship and often seeks to undermine those who have a role in leading worship.

If you are a worship leader or part of a worship team, you will be tested. Changing an atmosphere will require you to see the vision before you can experience the vision. You may feel like Ezekiel being placed in a dead place and told to declare life!

The hand of the LORD was upon me, and He brought me out by the Spirit of the LORD and set me down in the middle of the valley; and it was full of bones. He caused me to pass among them round about, and behold, there were very many on the surface of the valley; and lo, they were very dry.
(Ezekiel 37:1-2 NASB)

Only those with vision can survive in difficult, dreary, or depressing situations without being overwhelmed. Your vision on the inside must be bigger than the problem on the outside. In worship, we confront the atmosphere with praise and continue until the change is evident!

Imagine being placed into a valley full of dry bones and asked, *"Son of man, can these bones live?"* I felt death in some atmospheres where I have been asked to lead worship. I have endured the stares of death and the raised brows of many people who did not believe that life was possible.

However, You and I will be called to declare life in a graveyard- the last place life could be imagined. Ezekiel lifted up his voice in the place of death and the valley began to transform.

So I prophesied as I was commanded; and as I prophesied, there was a noise, and behold, a rattling; and the bones came together, bone to its bone. And I looked, and behold, sinews were on them, and flesh grew and skin covered them; but there was no breath in them. (Ezekiel 37:7-8 NASB)

Like Ezekiel, we must prophesy to depressing, hopeless situations instead of being overcome by them. The dry bones did not deter him from declaring life. The power behind the prophetic word is for this very purpose.

Words are containers that carry either faith or fear. When we gather to worship, the lyrics of our songs that we sing release either faith or fear into the atmosphere. If my heart is full of faith, I release faith through my words. If my heart is full of fear, I release fear with my words.

Do not be afraid to prophesy in stages. Ezekiel saw the bones come together, but also saw there was no breath in them. He realized the incompleteness of the work that needed to be done, and so God gave him the continuation of the prophetic word. Don't quit prophesying until the full manifestation occurs.

Then He said to me, "Prophesy to the breath, prophesy, son of man, and say to the breath, 'Thus says the Lord GOD, "Come from the four winds, O breath, and breathe on these slain, that they come to life."'" So I prophesied as He commanded me, and the breath came into them, and they came to life and stood on their feet, an exceedingly great army. (Ezekiel 37:9-10 NASB)

The prophetic word has the power to bring order. Notice His ordering of the bones preceded His manifestation of life. Order precedes life. Do not prophesy life until you first prophesy order!

As Ezekiel prophesied, there was a noise and rattling sound first. The prophetic word is often an alarm clock to a sleeping church. Many dislike the prophetic because it first comes as a rattling noise before it brings order and life!

God will send the four winds to *"...breathe into the slain that they may live."* As you worship you are ministering to those who are hurting, who have been slaughtered by the enemy, who are dead, dry and disordered. This is the calling of the prophet: to bring life to the lifeless, hope to the hopeless, and courage to the fearful.

As Ezekiel prophesied to the bones, they **"…came to life and stood up on their feet."** The prophetic word will establish, bring to life and bring back to their feet that which was dead and fallen. Note what was dead, dry, and disordered became ready, alive, and ordered through what was prophesied to them. The prophet must face the dismal situation, confront it with His word and then witness the transformation. The final product: a vast army! That is what is in the heart of God and that is the vision the prophet must carry within his or her heart. Prophets are militantly oriented, which is why they are often misunderstood and rejected. So let this militant orientation turn into your motivation to prophesy.

Prophecy and Music

King David understood the spiritual authority that is released through music. He set up times for the ministry to Yahweh His God because it was a key to his kingdom's success. David invested in the ministry of prophecy and worship.

David, together with the commanders of the army, set apart some of the sons of Asaph, Heman and Jeduthun for the ministry of prophesying, accompanied by harps, lyres and cymbals (1 Chronicles 25:1).

Sound is vibrating energy. Many scientists believe the smallest particles of matter are actually vibrating strings. This idea is called the "string theory". Vibrations are literally the substance of everything around us!

Now faith is being sure of what we hope for and certain of what we do not see. This is what the ancients were commended for. By faith we understand that the universe was formed at God's command, so that what is seen was not made out of what was visible. (Hebrews 11:1-3)

The idea that sound is the precursor to all that is visual is a

59

biblical concept. In the beginning God created the heavens and the earth by speaking a declaration. God said, "Let there be light," and it was! The sound of His voice brought into existence all that we see around us. God had a vision in his mind of what He wanted before He spoke. God created the visible world around us through His spoken word! We are created in His image and we can shift the atmosphere around us by what we speak.

There is an experiment you can see online where sand is placed on a thin piece of metal.[10] A speaker is placed next to the metal plate and various tones are played through the speaker. As each note is changed, the sand forms a different pattern on the metal plate!

Watching sand particles form shapes reminds me to be bold in my declaration. Unspoken, silent prayers may have a place but I don't want to miss out on aligning the atmosphere around me to the kingdom of God. God formed that which is visible through that which is audible; what is spoken is a precursor to that which is seen.

There is a story about military commander who was in the midst of a losing battle and decided that all was lost and he needed to sound the retreat. He motioned for the bugle boy who immediately ran to his side. The military commander told the bugle boy, "Young man, sound the retreat!" To his surprise the bugle boy responded, "Sir, I do not know how to sound the retreat." The commander said, "Well, what do you know how to sound?" "I only know how to sound the charge!" The commander then commissioned the bugle boy, "Sound the charge young man! Sound the charge!" As the bugle boy sounded the charge, the army was inspired and the troops turned the battle around to win the victory.

We need worshippers who do not know how to sound the retreat and know only how to sound the charge. We have authority to win every battle because of what Jesus has done for us.

---

[10] Check out http://www.youtube.com/watch?v=wio728lLOh0 for a video entitled "The Art of Sound".

Reflection

1. How did the king of Babylon weaken the cities that he conquered? Is Satan using the same method to weaken the church of Jesus Christ?
2. Consider a time in which you felt like you were placed in a graveyard and God told you to speak life.
3. God created the world around us through the sound of His voice. We are created in His image. Do you consider your voice to have creative power?
4. What are some worship songs that release faith over you as you sing? Do all worship songs that we sing release faith?
5. What does the statement "He who sings prays twice" mean to you?

Chapter 6
The Foundation
of Worship

W e cannot expect to build a tall building unless we first lay a
strong foundation. When a building is being constructed,
its shape and size are very much determined by the
foundation upon which it is erected. Worship is that foundation in
every believer's life.

For seventy years, the city of Jerusalem was left in ruins,
but as Daniel read the words of Jeremiah, he was stirred to pray
for the Jews to return to Jerusalem. Within a few years, those
prayers were answered and Jews began returning to the their
desolate city to rebuild their homes. Despite many fears and the
constant threats, the Jews laid the foundation for the temple and

then began to worship the LORD:

When the builders laid the foundation of the temple of the Lord, the priests in their vestments and with trumpets, and the Levites (the sons of Asaph) with cymbals, took their places to praise the Lord, as prescribed by David king of Israel. With praise and thanksgiving they sang to the Lord: "He is good; his love to Israel endures forever." And all the people gave a great shout of praise to the Lord, because the foundation of the house of the Lord was laid. (Ezra 3:10-11)

Before the walls were put in place around the city, the place of sacrifice was established. Ministry to God Himself was the priority as the Jews returned to Jerusalem. Reinstating the sacrifices for the pleasure of the LORD became their rallying point.

The church can become a place of ministry to people but it must first be a place of ministry to the LORD. The enemy is very good at distracting us from our foundations. Years later, Jesus entered this same temple that the Jews had risked their lives to build. When He entered the temple, he overturned tables and drove out those who were buying and selling there. Jesus cried out, *"My house will be called a house of prayer"* (Matthew 21:13). In all our religious activity, we must never leave our foundation of prayer and worship.

<u>Who</u> Are We Worshipping?

All worship culminates in the book of Revelation. Here we have a redeemed people, saved by the blood of Jesus, worshipping God and the Lamb with the Father sharing His throne with His Son Jesus Christ.

Then I saw in the right hand of him who sat on the throne a scroll with writing on both sides and sealed with seven seals. And I saw a mighty angel proclaiming in a loud voice, "Who is worthy to break the seals and open the scroll?" But no one

*in heaven or on earth or under the earth could open the scroll
or even look inside it. I wept and wept because no one was
found who was worthy to open the scroll or look inside. Then
one of the elders said to me, "Do not weep! See, the Lion of the
tribe of Judah, the Root of David, has triumphed. He is able
to open the scroll and its seven seals."* (Revelation 5:1-5)

Jesus is not only the Lamb who was slain but also the Lion
of the tribe of Judah! Our worship should be focused on the
Father and on Jesus His Son who sits beside Him upon the throne.
Throughout the Old Testament, God the Father used his personal
name to tell people who He was!

*God also said to Moses, "Say to the Israelites, 'The LORD
(Yahweh), the God of your fathers—the God of Abraham, the
God of Isaac and the God of Jacob—has sent me to you.' This
is my name forever, the name by which I am to be remembered
from generation to generation.* (Exodus 3:15)

Many Bible teachers teach that God has many names, but
in fact He has only one name forever. Translated from the
Hebrew, God said to Moses to the tell the Israelites, *"Yahweh (the
LORD) has sent me to you."* Most Bibles use the words 'the
LORD' to translate the name 'Yahweh'.

In my opinion, failing to translate God's personal name as
Yahweh has been the greatest translation failure in most of our
modern day Bibles! We sing "Yahweh, Yahweh" in our churches,
but most Christians have no idea to whom we are singing! We are
singing to the Father of Jesus and to our Heavenly Father!

One of the most common words we use in worship is
"Hallelujah". The Hebrew word *hallel* means *'to praise'* and *'yah'* is
short for Yahweh. Hallelujah is the exclamation *"Praise You
Yahweh!"* Yahweh is God Himself and Jesus is God's Son who
must be treated with the same honor as God Himself!

Moreover, the Father judges no one, but has entrusted all judgment to the Son, that all may honor the Son just as they honor the Father. He who does not honor the Son does not honor the Father, who sent him. (John 5:22-23)

You will not find the name of Yahweh in the New Testament. I was pondering on this one day and asked, *"Why isn't your name in the New Testament?"* I heard Him say, *"What do your children call you? Chris or Dad?"* I then realized God Himself prefers we call Him "Father" since we are now His children because of what Jesus has done!

I would encourage you in your worship to use God's name but to emphasize Him as Father. We worship before the throne on which Jesus is seated beside His Father. You may disagree with me theologically, but practically I try to avoid overcomplicated thought processes like the Trinity in worship. Yahweh is the name of our Heavenly Father and Jesus is the name of the one who lives in me and who is the Lord of my life.

I have concluded in my understanding that worship belongs to God and to the Lamb! Jesus shed His blood so that all nations would worship the God of Israel. Yahweh never intended to be the God of only one nation. *"All the nations you have made will come and worship before you, O Lord; they will bring glory to your name"* (Psalm 86:9).

I love to sing songs that shout, "Yahweh, Yahweh" in fulfillment of these verses in the Bible. The God of Israel is now the God of all nations and His Son Jesus made this possible. For the Jews, they must recognize Jesus alongside of Yahweh in their worship. His ascension to the throne is seen in one of Daniel's visions:

In my vision at night I looked, and there before me was one like a son of man, coming with the clouds of heaven. He approached the Ancient of Days and was led into his presence. He was given authority, glory and sovereign power; all peoples, nations and men of every language worshiped him. His

dominion is an everlasting dominion that will not pass away,
and his kingdom is one that will never be destroyed.
(Daniel 7:13-14)

By glorifying and recognizing Jesus we glorify the Father. We worship before the throne of God and the Lamb, exalting Father and Son, joining with Jews and non-Jews in worship. John sees this picture in his vision:

After this I looked and there before me was a great multitude
that no one could count, from every nation, tribe, people and
language, standing before the throne and in front of the Lamb.
They were wearing white robes and were holding palm branches
in their hands. And they cried out in a loud voice: "Salvation
belongs to our God, who sits on the throne, and to the Lamb."
(Revelations 7:9-10)

The book of Revelation is a picture of men purchased for God by the blood of Jesus who are rejoicing exceedingly around the throne. We are spectacularly favored by a God who is extremely gracious! The foundation of our praise must is based upon Jesus' great sacrifice for us.

Jesus had to redirect the reason of rejoicing in the hearts of His disciples. *"However, do not rejoice that the spirits submit to you, but rejoice that your names are written in heaven"* (Luke 10:20). The foundation of our worship must be that our names are written in heaven. Our joy cannot be based upon whether or not our names are in the news, in books, on paychecks, or even on a marriage certificate. Our joy flows out of our names being written in the Book of Life. Jesus said about those who overcome, *"I will never blot out his name from the book of life, but will acknowledge his name before my Father and his angels"* (Revelation 3:5).

When we base our worship from an eternal perspective we will always worship. When our foundation relies on feelings, people or circumstances we will not be able to overcome the world, the flesh and the devil through our worship. Our songs should spring forth because of what the LORD has done and a faith that cries out, "Do it again God!"

Worship the Lamb

The Chinese language is a very artistic and pictorial language. The characters of the alphabet are pictures of objects and symbols. The ancient Chinese combined symbols to make up compound characters in order to express complex ideas.

Many scholars have discovered that the first eleven chapters of Genesis are the storyline behind the development of many of the basic symbols of the Chinese language. I believe that after the scattering following the Tower of Babel, a group left Babel and headed east toward what is now China. Their language was based upon the ideas they held in common before they left Babel. For instance, the Chinese character for "to covet or desire" combines of a picture of woman and a picture of two trees.[11]

Both Chinese culture and the Bible relate sheep to *personal* sacrifice and redemption. These attributes are the same as those of God's sacrificial Lamb: the Lord Jesus Christ.

©www.Bible.ca

義 =	羊 +	我 (	手 +	戈)
Righteousness	Sheep	Me	Hand	Knife

The character that means righteousness in Chinese consists of a sheep that is placed on top of 'me' and suggests that each individual has to make a personal choice to gain righteousness through the sacrificial sheep.

The world will become happy when we worship God and the Lamb! Happiness is the character for God and the character for sheep combined together! Sounds like the book of Revelation!

---

[11] The Discovery of Genesis, Ethel R. Nelson, location 1031

No longer will there be any curse. The throne of God and of the Lamb will be in the city, and his servants will serve him. They will see his face, and his name will be on their foreheads. There will be no more night. They will not need the light of a lamp or the light of the sun, for the Lord God will give them light. And they will reign for ever and ever. (Revelations 22:3-5)

Worship happens before God when we place ourselves under the Lamb. When John the Baptist saw Jesus, he cried out, *"Look, the Lamb of God, who takes away the sin of the world!"* (John 1:29). Jesus is worshipped throughout eternity as the Lamb who was slain. Happiness comes when we worship God and the Lamb.

Righteousness comes when we place ourselves under the Lamb who was slain. When we are trying to achieve righteousness through our own works, we are no longer covered by the Lamb. When we perceive righteousness is of our own doing, we often become complacent in our worship.

Complacency is a feeling of smug or uncritical satisfaction with oneself or one's achievements. Many churches lack passion in their worship because they feel they have attained their own righteousness. Complacency is the brother of self-righteousness. Passionate worship is fueled by our need of salvation and by having our eyes fixed upon the Lamb who provided it for us.

Revelation culminates with the co-rule of the Father and the Son. We will worship before the throne of God and the Lamb forever and ever! We will never get bored bowing down in thankfulness to the God who loved us! The sacrifice of the Lamb will never lose its preeminence in our hearts!

And I saw what looked like a sea of glass mixed with fire and, standing beside the sea, those who had been victorious over the beast and his image and over the number of his name. They held harps given them by God and sang the song of Moses the servant of God and the song of the Lamb: "Great and marvelous are your deeds, Lord God Almighty. Just and true are your ways, King of the ages. Who will not fear you, O Lord, and bring glory to your name? For you alone are holy. All nations will come and worship before you, for your righteous acts have been revealed." (Revelation 15:2-4)

Heaven will sing the song of Moses and the song of the Lamb. Those in heaven didn't stop singing the Song of Moses once the Lamb was slain. Moses declared this song in Deuteronomy 32 and it speaks of the character of Yahweh. The song declares His love, His wrath and His soon to be released justice upon the earth. The song of Moses may also refer to victory song the Israelites sang as the Red Sea came crashing down on Pharaoh and his armies:

Then Moses and the Israelites sang this song to the LORD: "I will sing to the LORD, for he is highly exalted. The horse and its rider he has hurled into the sea. (Exodus 15:1)

The song of Moses is the declaration of victory over Pharaoh and the song of the Lamb is our victory over sin and the devil! Both songs declare a victory brought about by the blood of the Lamb. The Israelites were delivered by the blood of the Passover Lamb and we have been delivered by Jesus, the Lamb of God!

Priestly Praise

Priests are those who give their lives to offer up sacrifice to God. The church is a kingdom of priests who serve God and who will reign on the earth. The priests come with a blood sacrifice, the Lamb who was slain, singing a new song:

And they sang a new song: "You are worthy to take the scroll and to open its seals, because you were slain, and with your blood you purchased men for God from every tribe and language and people and nation. You have made them to be a kingdom and priests to serve our God, and they will reign on the earth." (Revelation 5:9-10)

God's purpose for mankind was to have a people who would function as priests. Yahweh spoke His desire to the nation of Israel:

And ye shall be unto me a kingdom of priests, and an holy nation. These are the words which thou shalt speak unto the children of Israel. (Exodus 19:6 KJV)

The word for priest in Hebrew is *kohen* comes from a root meaning *"a base, such as the base of a column."*[12] The priests are the structure support of the community. It is their responsibility to keep the community standing tall and straight, a sign of righteousness. God desired all the Israelites to be set apart for His purposes on the earth.

For thou art an holy people unto the LORD thy God, and the LORD hath chosen thee to be a peculiar people unto himself, above all the nations that are upon the earth.
(Deuteronomy 14:2 KJV)

Peculiar usually means *"to be strange, odd or unusual"*. If you have been in church lately, that is a good definition! The fellowship I have pastored for the last several years has a sign on

---

[12] Benner, Jeff A. The Ancient Hebrew Language and Alphabet: Understanding the Ancient Hebrew Language of the Bible Based on Ancient Hebrew Culture and Thought. College Station, TX: Virtualbookworm. Com Pub., 2004. Print.

our wall that says, "No More Church as Usual". I believe the church, the body of Christ, ought to be colorful and unique. The word for peculiar, though in this verse is not referring to this idea.

The word for peculiar in Hebrew is *segullah* and is defined as *"personal property, treasured possession...which one has personally acquired and carefully preserved"*.[13] The word signifies a private possession that one has personally acquired and has been carefully preserved. Peculiar means that we exclusively belong to our God. Yahweh was seeking a people of whom He could say, *"You are mine!"*

Yahweh also desired a holy people. The word *"holy,"* or *kadosh* in Hebrew, is usually applied to a righteous or pious person who becomes holy through their actions and avoidance of sin. But *kadosh* points to an act or state in which people or things are set aside and reserved exclusively for God. They must be withheld from ordinary use and treated with special care as something that belongs to God. I like to define holy as to be devoted *to* something or someone.

I graduated from Penn State University with a degree in Hotel, Restaurant and Institutional Management. Whenever I was overseeing a kitchen, I had to be sure we separated certain cutting boards for raw meats and others for non-cooked food items. We had red color-coded cutting boards that were easily identified and were only to be used for raw meats. We could say the red cutting boards were holy and to be set apart only for raw meats.

In our lives, we must make separations between holy and common. God's first act was to create, but His second act was to separate.

In the beginning God created the heavens and the earth. Now the earth was formless and empty, darkness was over the surface of the deep, and the Spirit of God was hovering over the waters. And God said, "Let there be light," and there was

---

[13] Zodhiates, Spiros, and John R. Kohlenberger. *The Hebrew-Greek Key Study Bible: New International Version*. Chattanooga, TN: AMG Pub.1996. 1536

light. God saw that the light was good, and he separated the light from the darkness. (Genesis 1:1-4)

Because art is a powerful force that commands influence in society, creativity must be mixed with an ability to distinguish between good and evil, holy and common. Yahweh warned His people, *"You must distinguish between the holy and the common, between the unclean and the clean"* (Leviticus 10:10). BADAL is the Hebrew word that means *"to separate or divide either literally or figuratively, to make a distinction."* [14]

In the world they say, *"Write drunk, edit sober!"* In the kingdom I say, *"Write drunk in the Spirit, but edit soberly and in the fear of the LORD."* Submit what you create to godly people in your life and have them prayerfully go over your work. Satan wants to break down the separation of good and evil. God created and then got a vision of what was good so that He could separate it. As creators, we should follow the pattern God has set as an example for us. One pattern will end in blessing; the other in bondage:

Kingdom of God
1. Creation of Situation
2. Vision of Good
3. Separation
4. Blessing

Kingdom of Darkness
1. Creation of Situation
2. Deception
3. Unifying Good and Evil
4. Bondage

The author of Hebrews says, *"But solid food is for the mature, who by constant use have trained themselves to distinguish good from evil"* (Hebrews 5:14). Maturity is based upon our ability to separate good from evil. Christian artists who submit themselves to their spiritual authorities will develop the maturity and training needed to distinguish between what is holy

---

[14] Ibid. p. 1506

and what is common.

Priests were responsible to bring suitable offerings to be sacrificed. Yahweh rebuked the priests in the times of Malachi.

"A son honors his father, and a slave his master. If I am a father, where is the honor due me? If I am a master, where is the respect due me?" says the Lord Almighty. "It is you priests who show contempt for my name." But you ask, "How have we shown contempt for your name?" "By offering defiled food on my altar." (Malachi 1:6-7)

All worship leaders are priests who are to make holy offerings before God throughout eternity. The priests in the times of Malachi were offering blind, lame, and diseased animal sacrifices that were not acceptable for any king. Justly indignant, Yahweh held the leaders of their day accountable for their improper sacrifices, and I am sure He still receives lame worship offerings. Help us give God what He desires!

Everyday, we should pray for and receive daily bread. I remember early in my married life, when our income was limited, we would occasionally buy day-old donuts. These were nice treats for our family until one day my brother visited me. On his way to our house, he picked up fresh donuts. Though these donuts looked and felt the same, the moment I took my first bite I experienced the taste of fresh! Fresh invigorates all those who experience it, and as priests we must not become satisfied with day-old bread. As we receive our daily bread, we are no longer an echo; we are a voice.

But ye are a chosen generation, a royal priesthood, an holy nation, a peculiar people; that ye should shew forth the praises of him who hath called you out of darkness into his marvelous light. (1 Peter 2:9-10 KJV)

Priests understand the power of worship to help bring reconciliation between heaven and earth. Every priest should continually declare the praises of He who sits on the throne and unto the Lamb. Worship is the one activity that we will do in both this life and the next, and we never need to base our worship on feeling or present circumstances. The foundation of our worship is based upon what Jesus has done and our confidence in what He accomplished. Eternity is just the beginning! Let us join with John the apostle and declare:

To him who loves us and has freed us from our sins by his blood, and has made us to be a kingdom and priests to serve his God and Father—to him be glory and power for ever and ever! Amen. (Revelation 1:5-7)

Heaven is wherever Jesus is, and heaven is coming to Earth. The ground beneath your feet will one day be under the complete rule of God the Father and His Son Jesus. Those who acknowledge Jesus as Lord will experience a celebration that no one eye has seen, no ear has heard, and no mind could comprehend. Our worship times are mere rehearsals for what is yet to come.

Reflection

1. The book of Revelations ends with those in heaven worshipping at the throne of God and the Lamb. Who is God? Who is the Lamb?
2. We are called to be a priesthood that is holy. What is the meaning of the Hebrew word *kadosh?*
3. Define complacency? How does this attitude affect our worship?
4. What should be the foundation of our worship? What did the Jews do first when they returned to Jerusalem in the book of Ezra?
5. When the Bible calls those who follow Jesus "a peculiar people", what would be the best definition of the word peculiar in this context?

Chapter 7
Freedom to
Worship

The Israelites were slaves in Egypt until God raised up a deliver by the name of Moses. True freedom is the freedom to worship. God raised up a deliver for Israel and now He has raised up a deliver for you and me! His name is Jesus and He is risen!

Deliverance came to Israel so that they could worship. The sign that God was with them would be shown to them through their liberty to worship Him.

And God said, "I will be with you. And this will be the sign to you that it is I who have sent you: When you have brought the people out of Egypt, you will worship God on this mountain." (Eoxdus 3:12)

The same idea holds true today. One of the most visible signs of a person who is free is their ability to worship. There are times when I do not feel free, so I begin to dance before the

LORD, as a prophetic act, declaring complete freedom.

Imagine as Moses sees the bush on fire wondering to himself, *"Who is this God who is before me?"* Moses wanted to know who was speaking to him.

Moses said to God, "Suppose I go to the Israelites and say to them, 'The God of your fathers has sent me to you,' and they ask me, 'What is his name?' Then what shall I tell them?" God said to Moses, "I am who I am. This is what you are to say to the Israelites: 'I am has sent me to you.'" God also said to Moses, "Say to the Israelites, 'The Lord, the God of your fathers—the God of Abraham, the God of Isaac and the God of Jacob—has sent me to you.' This is my name forever, the name by which I am to be remembered from generation to generation. (Exodus 3:12-15)

The name of God is not I AM. I AM was a statement of His reality in the present. His name is Yahweh for all generations. He is the Father of Jesus. When Moses arrived in Egypt, he had one message to Pharaoh: "We are going to have a festival to Yahweh for three days."

Opposition to Worship

We should not be shocked that we face opposition when we set our hearts on radical worship. Satan understands the power we have been given in worship and will oppose us just as Pharaoh opposed Moses. God wanted His people to worship Him and sent Moses to tell the most powerful person on earth what to do.

Afterward Moses and Aaron went to Pharaoh and said, "This is what the Lord, the God of Israel, says: 'Let my people go, so that they may hold a festival to me in the desert.'"
(Exodus 5:1)

The Israelites were slaves in Egypt at this time. They

worked for Pharaoh building the pyramids. The pyramids were triangular shaped structures created to house the dead bodies of Egypt's kings. Egyptians believed in the afterlife and felt that by having a nice place to be buried guaranteed a great afterlife. Many of the Pharaoh's even had living servants sealed in with them in their tombs.

Moses was commanding that Pharaoh release the bulk of his workforce to spend time worshipping Yahweh. Pharaoh's first response to Moses' request was to accuse the Israelites of being lazy. Pharaoh told his supervisors:

Require them to make the same number of bricks as before (without providing them with straw); don't reduce the quota. They are lazy; that is why they are crying out, 'Let us go and sacrifice to our God.' Make the work harder for the men so that they keep working and pay no attention to lies." (Exodus 5:8-9 *italics mine)*

The enemy likes to classify worship as unproductive time spent. Many of us still hear Pharaoh's voice when we are worshipping. We must embrace our worship as our work before God and His Son Jesus. Jesus Himself addresses the work versus worship controversy when He walked the planet. Jesus was welcomed into the house of Mary and Martha and as He began to teach, Martha continued working. Mary, on the other hand, sat at His feet listening.

Scripture says, *"Martha was distracted by all the preparations that had to be made"* (Luke 10:40). *A distraction is something that prevents someone from giving full attention to something else.* The work that needed to be done became the ideal distraction to Martha. She then vented her frustrations to Jesus: *"Lord, don't you care that my sister has left me to do the work by myself? Tell her to help me!"* (vs.40).

When I read the Scriptures, I often consider all the different responses Jesus could have given at that moment. I often consider what I would have said were I in that situation. I must confess that I probably would have sided with Martha! Hear how Jesus responded to the situation:

"Martha, Martha," the Lord answered, "you are worried and upset about many things, but few things are needed—or indeed only one. Mary has chosen what is better, and it will not be taken away from her." (Luke 10:39-42)

Jesus took the side of Mary without any consolation toward Martha. Worship is the one thing that is needed and Mary chose what was best. We must chose worship over work even in the face of accusations of laziness!

We must continually remind ourselves that God does not need our work. An angel could proclaim the gospel to the lost if needed. An entire village could be visited by Jesus in a dream and be saved. Our work is not needed as much as we may think! We are privileged to work for God, but it can become a distraction to the one thing needed: WORSHIP!

Uncompromised Worship

The story of Moses delivering the people of Israel from Egypt reminds us that our enemies are willing to compromise. We serve the Most High God, and what He commands us to do, He will back us up by His authority. Uncompromised obedience to God's commands is our job: the results are God's job.

Moses tells Pharaoh that the Israelites are to go on a three-day journey into the wilderness where they will worship their God Yahweh. Pharaoh resists Moses' request until the Nile is turned to blood and then a plague of frogs hits his nations. He responds:

Pharaoh summoned Moses and Aaron and said, "Pray to the Lord to take the frogs away from me and my people, and I will let your people go to offer sacrifices to the Lord." (Exodus 8:8)

Ten plagues strike Egypt in this story because of Pharaoh's

refusal to let Israel worship in the way in which Yahweh commanded them. Pharaoh offers Moses three compromises that we should note in this story.

1. Compromise #1: You can worship without leaving Egypt.

Then Pharaoh summoned Moses and Aaron and said, "Go, sacrifice to your God here in the land" (Exodus 8:25). Yahweh commanded the Israelites to go into the wilderness, but Pharaoh was only willing to have them worship in Egypt.

2. Compromise #2: Men *only,* not households, can worship.

Then Moses and Aaron were brought back to Pharaoh. "Go, worship the Lord your God," he said. "But just who will be going?" Moses answered, "We will go with our young and old, with our sons and daughters, and with our flocks and herds, because we are to celebrate a festival to the Lord." Pharaoh said, "The Lord be with you—if I let you go, along with your women and children! Clearly you are bent on evil. No! Have only the men go; and worship the Lord, since that's what you have been asking for." Then Moses and Aaron were driven out of Pharaoh's presence. (Exodus 10:8-11)

3. Compromise #3: You can worship, but without sacrifice.

Then Pharaoh summoned Moses and said, "Go, worship the Lord. Even your women and children may go with you; only leave your flocks and herds behind." But Moses said, "You must allow us to have sacrifices and burnt offerings to present to the Lord our God. Our livestock too must go with us; not a hoof is to be left behind. We have to use some of them in worshiping the Lord our God, and until we get there we will not know what we are to use to worship the Lord." But the Lord hardened Pharaoh's heart, and he was not willing to let them go. (Exodus 10:24-27)

The Israelites were brought into freedom because their leader would not compromise where worship was concerned. Pharaoh was willing to let them go without their wives and children, without sacrifice and without leaving Egypt, but Moses said, "No deal!" It was Yahweh or No Way!

Uncompromised worship brought the Israelites out of bondage in Egypt to the Promise Land. When we stop compromising our worship stance, the enemy is judged and true freedom comes into our lives.

Expressions of Worship

One thing I have learned in over twenty-five years of leading worship is that many people do not like to be told to do something. Some worshippers are submissive when asked to raise their hands or shout out. Others feel that if they are told to do something it is not coming from their hearts. As I lead worship, I invite others into the presence of God through various expressions.

Early in my ministry, I would bark out commands to my congregation in the way God was leading me. I would tell the people to shout, to sing and to dance. One a woman complained to my pastor saying, *"I felt like we were being pushed into worship today!"* He kindly responded, *"Why were you resisting?"*

I have discovered that my zealous style of leading was not always what worked best. *Good leaders lead people into His presence.* Some people are good worshippers but not good leaders. Others are good leaders but poor worshippers. If you desire to lead people into His courts with praise you must be both a good leader and a good worshipper.

There are many different ways to express our worship to God. These expressions are often prophetic or symbolic acts that the Bible describes as protocol to enter into His presence. If we express our worship in these Biblical ways, we should expect to experience His presence.

Some would argue that His presence comes if our hearts are right with Him. The truth is that if our hearts are right with Him, we should be responding in a Biblical manner! Jesus spoke these words about His generation:

To what, then, can I compare the people of this generation? What are they like? They are like children sitting in the marketplace and calling out to each other: "We played the flute for you, and you did not dance; we sang a dirge, and you did not cry." (Luke 7:31-32)

Worship demands a response! Sometimes the response may be silence and awe but other times the response may be shouting, clapping and dancing. God's goodness will do something inside of us, spilling out of us in some kind of expression.

Scripture offers many different expressions in worship that will help us get our breakthrough in life. Sometimes words are not enough when we are feeling overwhelmed or depressed. There is potential power in every act of worship that will leave a residue of strength for daily life.

Lifting Your Hands

David could have just spoken his prayers. But I am sure he felt a greater sense of power when He prayed to God with uplifted hands. *"Hear my cry for mercy as I call to you for help, as I lift up my hands toward your Most Holy Place"* (Psalm 28:2). Lifting one's hands is a sign of surrender to God—opening up and becoming vulnerable to His presence.

Consider the story of Moses as He sent His army commander Joshua into battle. Moses stretched out his hands and victory ensued.

So Joshua fought the Amalekites as Moses had ordered, and Moses, Aaron and Hur went to the top of the hill. As long as Moses held up his hands, the Israelites were winning, but whenever he lowered his hands, the Amalekites were winning. When Moses' hands grew tired, they took a stone and put it under him and he sat on it. Aaron and Hur held his hands up—one on one side, one on the other—so that his hands remained steady till sunset. So Joshua overcame the Amalekite army with the sword. (Exodus 17:10-13)

The power of outstretched arms is a prophetic sign that God is bringing you victory. We often lift up our hands, but to stretch them up to heaven is a sign of reaching out to our Heavenly Father. We may be facing difficult trials or be in an impossible situation. When Moses was trapped between the Pharaoh's army and the Red Sea, the LORD told him to stop whining and start stretching out your hands!

Raise your staff and stretch out your hand over the sea to divide the water so that the Israelites can go through the sea on dry ground. (Exodus 14:16)

There is a grace released in the atmosphere as we worship with uplifted hands. *"I will praise you as long as I live, and in your name I will lift up my hands"* (Psalm 63:4) and, *"Lift up your hands in the sanctuary and praise the Lord"* (Psalm 134:2). When our arms are stretched out before God, this visible act of worship moves mountains standing in our way.

Musical Instruments in Worship

The Bible clearly teaches that musical instruments are more than merely things that are played to accompany worship; they are in and of themselves praise to God:

Praise him with the sounding of the trumpet...with the harp and lyre, with tambourine and dancing...with the strings and flute...with the clash of cymbals...with resounding cymbals.
(Psalm 150:3-5)

I used to believe that worship was powerful because it conveyed a truth expressed through words. I assumed someone had to be singing for the song to be a worship song. I have now learned that true worship can happen without a word being spoken!

There is an instrumental song that is on one of the first Vineyard Music CD's. The song is actually a recording at the end of a service at a conference. The melodies played on this recording ministered deeply to my spirit beyond what words could ever do. The sounds on that instrumental released a healing in my spirit man that I will never forget.

Remember when David played his harp Saul got delivered from evil spirits? Spiritual power resided in the strumming of those strings. God is calling skillful musicians to release deliverance over those who are being held captive by evil spirits.

Sing joyfully to the Lord, you righteous; it is fitting for the upright to praise him. Praise the LORD with the harp; make music to him on the ten-stringed lyre. Sing to him a new song; play skillfully, and shout for joy (Psalms 33:1-3).

Some Christians question how much skill is required to be used as a vessel in worship. I have pondered the same thought throughout my years as a worship leader. I have come to the conclusion that skill is one requirement for anyone desiring to lead in worship or even being part of a worship team.

Playing skillfully should be a goal for every person desiring to serve in worship. I want to be a great worshipper! To be a great worshipper I must therefore be a good musician. When someone on the team fails to play the proper notes at the proper time, the music distracts us instead of enhancing our worship. When everyone on the team is well rehearsed, it honors God and brings forth a united song. Psalm 33 reminds us to play skillfully; Psalm 133 reminds us of how good and blessed it is to play in unity.

How good and pleasant it is when God's people live together in unity! It is like precious oil poured on the head, running down on the beard running down on Aaron's beard, down on the collar of his robe. It is as if the dew of Hermon were falling on Mount Zion. For there the Lord bestows his blessing, even life forevermore (Psalm 133:1-3).

God is calling a people out of bondage and into worship. The Pharaohs of our day will offer compromises we must refuse. In the next chapter, we will discuss how worship releases spiritual authority over our lives and how we can be prepared in worship for this battle.

Reflection

1. What did Jesus say to Martha was the one thing that was needed?

2. What are compromises that we make in our worship? In what ways was Pharaoh willing to compromise?

3. Do you consider the playing of instruments a form of praise? Have you limited worship to the words being sung over the music?

4. Instead of lifting your hands in praise try stretching them out before the LORD. Do you feel the difference?

5. Is it important to play an instrument with skill to be a good worshipper? Is skill the only quality that is needed?

Chapter 8

How To Survive an Attack

Many of us have had the experience of reaching our destination only to discover we failed to pack a certain necessity! This chapter is a packing guide for the journey that is ahead of you. Worship is a provision for your spirit that is more important than bread or water.

Jesus went out on a wilderness journey and did not fail to pack the necessary tools for survival. After fasting in the wilderness for forty days, the devil began to tempt Him. The last thing Jesus said to the devil was: *"Away from me, Satan! For it is written: 'Worship the Lord your God, and serve him only'"* (Matthew 4:10). When we focus our lives on worshipping and serving God alone, we will experience the same victory that Jesus experienced: *"Then the devil left him, and angels came and attended him"* (Matthew 4:11).

When we worship and serve the LORD only, we begin to see things as they really are. Our understanding of *who Jesus is* and *who we are* becomes crystal clear. When Jesus was in the wilderness, Satan began with the question, *"If you are the Son of God..."* (Matthew 4:3). Notice our enemy attempts to bring doubt upon our relationship with our Heavenly Father. Once we begin to doubt, we no longer feel like ourselves. Believing in who God said you are and the relationship you have with Him is what makes you a candidate to receive grace from the Father. James reminds us of this truth:

But when you ask, you must believe and not doubt, because the one who doubts is like a wave of the sea, blown and tossed by the wind. That person should not expect to receive anything from the Lord. Such a person is double-minded and unstable in all they do. (James 1:6-8)

Once we know who we are, we can begin to walk in the power of the kingdom of God. This kingdom exists wherever the king is worshipped and obeyed without doubt or hesitation.

Entering the Promise Land

Jesus came to be the new Joshua. Joshua took the Israelites into the Promised Land to establish the kingdom of Israel. This land had giants that needed to have their heads chopped off. They were intimidating and big and unwilling to leave. But God had given the land of Israel to the Israelites. They had to take their swords and conquer.

The Bible calls praise a double-edged sword. *"May the praise of God be in their mouths and a double-edged sword in their hands..."*(Psalm 149:6). Praise is a double-edged sword because it is a word spoken both in heaven and on earth. God said it, so when we declare what God has spoken, it becomes a doubled-edged sword in our hand.

The Israelites were called out of Egypt to conquer the land

of Promise. God is calling us to take our Promised Land as well; therefore, we must have promises that we are expecting to receive. Too many Christians forget that the Promised Land is inhabited with giants who want us to feel small. Demons are the inhabitants of our Promised Lands that need to be driven out and destroyed.

> *See, the LORD your God has given you the land. Go up and take possession of it as the LORD, the God of your fathers, told you. Do not be afraid; do not be discouraged.*
> (Deuteronomy 1:21)

The word for *'possess'* in Hebrew is the word *yarash*. It means to not only to take possession but also to dispossess and drive out the current occupants.[15] Taking authority over demons is the job that Jesus has delegated to us in the kingdom.

Symptoms of A Demonic Attack

None of us are immune to a demonic attack. The devil seeks to come at an opportune time, and many Christians are unfamiliar of the symptoms of a demonic attack. I want to share with you a few symptoms that will result in the diagnosis of an attack on your spirit.

1) **Loss of identity** (You do not feel yourself and often resort to masking yourself)

2) **Loss of Strength** (You are struggling to get through your day and feel overwhelmed)

3) **Loss of Hunger for God** (You do not feeling a desire to fellowship, prayer, ministry, reading the Bible)

4) **Loss or Distortion of Vision** (You are unmotivated or discouraged about the future)

5) **Loss or Distortion of Value** (You forget the value of forgiveness, our victory in Christ, the people around you,

---

[15] Zodhiates, Spiros, and John R. Kohlenberger. *The Hebrew-Greek Key Study Bible: New International Version*. Chattanooga, TN: AMG Pub.1996. 1521

your past victories and who you are to the kingdom of God)

When we look at how Jesus operated when under a spiritual attack, we learn that He used the word of God as His sword. Demonic attacks usually come at us with lies about our identity and destiny. We are not afraid of the devil, but rather we rule over him. We are aware of his schemes, but not obsessed with fear. Satan only has authority where we allow his lies to influence our thoughts and actions.

Eight Demonic Spirits

As we set apart our lives in obedience and in worship, we will be confronting different spirits at different times. Each spirit carries with it different characteristics. Satan's greatest tool is to disguise himself as an angel of light. We need to recognize the work of demonic spirits and not be deceived. Here is a list of evil spirits and how they operate:

1. The Spirit of the Anti-Christ –
Resists the Father and Jesus

Who is the liar? It is the man who denies that Jesus is the Christ. Such a man is the antichrist—he denies the Father and the Son. (1 John 2:22)

The word Anti-Christ is never mentioned in the book of Revelations and is only mentioned in four passages, all found in 1 John and 2 John. Most Christians believe the Anti-Christ is a person that will arise near the end of the ages, but scriptures point to the Anti-Christ as a spirit.

Dear friends, do not believe every spirit, but test the spirits to see whether they are from God, because many false prophets have gone out into the world. This is how you can recognize the Spirit of God: Every spirit that acknowledges that Jesus

Christ has come in the flesh is from God, but every spirit that does not acknowledge Jesus is not from God. This is the spirit of the antichrist, which you have heard is coming and even now is already in the world. (1 John 4:1-3)

I would encourage all believers to mindful of using the name of God's Son Jesus. Acknowledging Jesus and all that He has done for us glorifies the Father. The spirit of the Anti-Christ wants to quench the wonderful name of Jesus. John continually warned his listeners about the importance of acknowledging Jesus.

But every spirit that does not acknowledge Jesus is not from God. This is the spirit of the antichrist, which you have heard is coming and even now is already in the world. (1 John 4:3)

2. The Spirit of Heaviness-
Resists Praise, Joy and Fun

To appoint unto them that mourn in Zion, to give unto them beauty for ashes, the oil of joy for mourning, the garment of praise for the spirit of heaviness. (Isaiah 61:3)

God commands celebration. We come down hard on those who do not follow God's commandments. The ""do's" and the "do not's" are commands to be followed. Celebration is often a forgotten practice amongst Christians. We are much like the people in Nehemiah's time who God had to tell to stop the crying and start partying.

Nehemiah said, "Go and enjoy choice food and sweet drinks, and send some to those who have nothing prepared. This day is sacred to our Lord. Do not grieve, for the joy of the LORD is your strength." The Levites calmed all the people, saying, "Be still, for this is a sacred day. Do not grieve." Then all the people went away to eat and drink, to send portions of food and to celebrate with great joy, because they now understood the words that had been made known to them. (Nehemiah 8:10-13)

Great wrath will come upon those who will not celebrate— what a blessed threat! Learning how to party like God desires is what this writing is all about. We celebrate to remember our past and to look forward to our future.

The spirit of Heaviness is broken by the garment of praise. Sometimes I picture praise as a garment that I wear and see it as something I need to put on everyday. I sometimes wonder if some Christians wear it with the tag still on it just in case they want to return it! Our garment of praise must be worn continually.

3. The Spirit of Jezebel-
Resists Authority and Freedom

It my experience, it seems the Jezebel spirit can operate in both men and women. This spirit opposes God-given authority but often appears as very spiritual.

Nevertheless, I have this against you: You tolerate that woman Jezebel, who calls herself a prophet. By her teaching she misleads my servants into sexual immorality and the eating of food sacrificed to idols. (Revelation 2:20)

4. The Spirit of Leviathan-
Resists Truth and Light

Can you pull in Leviathan with a fishhook or tie down its tongue with a rope? Can you put a cord through its nose or pierce its jaw with a hook? Will it keep begging you for mercy? Will it speak to you with gentle words? Will it make an agreement with you for you to take it as your slave for life? Can you make a pet of it like a bird or put it on a leash for the young women in your house? Will traders barter for it? Will they divide it up among the merchants? Can you fill its hide with harpoons or its head with fishing spears? If you lay a hand on it, you will remember the struggle and never do it again! (Job 41:1-8)

The spirit of Leviathan is one of the most powerful spirits I have ever dealt with in my ministry. Leviathan comes from the root word "levi" meaning to be joined to or attached. This spirit weaves its way into every area of ministry to control and manipulate and begins to squeeze the life out of our spiritual life.

5. The Spirit of Mammon-
Resists Financial Giving
The body of Christ needs to invest in creative arts to reach the world with the message of Jesus Christ. The spirit of Mammon opposes generosity and lavish sacrifice. I have seen many worship teams with out-of-date sound systems and equipment because the spirit of Mammon controlled the finances of the church.

6. The Spirit of Python-
Resists Prayer and Freedom
The spirit of Python is a spirit that attempts to suffocate the message of the gospel. Paul and Silas were confronted with this spirit in the book of Acts:

And it came to pass in our going on to prayer, a certain maid, having a spirit of Python, did meet us. This girl followed Paul and the rest of us, shouting, "These men are servants of the Most High God, who are telling you the way to be saved." She kept this up for many days. (Acts 16:17 Young's Literal Translation)

Notice that Paul and Silas were on their way to prayer and this girl began to shout a true statement! Paul and Silas were declaring the way to be saved. Most spirits attack from the mouth and in a frontal attack but the spirit of Python operates in a subtle

93

manner, slowly suffocating a ministry or minister in attempts to destroy it. Note that this spirit followed Paul for many days.

Most snakes kill their victims through poison that is released through their fangs, but the python kills its prey by squeezing and suffocating its victim. The death process is not through poisoning but squeezing! This demonic spirit works slowly squeezing and stealing the breathe out of your life. If you have ever felt suffocated you are probably dealing with the Python spirit.

Even though the slave girl spoke truth about the kingdom, the spirit of Python filled her words. I heard a story from someone I know who attended a concert of a famous Christian pop singer. They said after the concert, even though she sang about Jesus, they were almost overcome by a spirit of lust. I believe, though her words were in line with scripture, she was operating under a different spirit.

The spirit of Python is discerned by a troubling in your spirit. You can't quite put your finger on it, but you know something is not quite right. The slave girl exclaimed truth: *"These men are servants of the Most High God, who are telling you the way to be saved."* Paul knew by his spirit that something was not right.

Do not be deceived by the spirit of Python! We must not rationalize what is said and discern a situation through merely our minds. If we are in Christ, our spirit will discern a different spirit in operation. We must remember that Satan is very good at masking himself as an angel of light. We must also be bold enough to act on what we are discerning. Paul felt troubled in his spirit and it took him many days to finally cast the spirit out of the girl.

Finally Paul became so troubled that he turned around and said to the spirit, "In the name of Jesus Christ I command you to come out of her!" At that moment the spirit left her. (Acts 16:18)

After Paul and Silas saw this girl set free, all hell broke

loose around them! The entire town turned on them and had them thrown into jail. They were stripped, beaten, severely flogged and chained up as criminals, yet they made a choice on that day to cry out to God in worship. Don't let the spirit of Python steal your praise! Look to Paul and Silas' example!

After they had been severely flogged, they were thrown into prison, and the jailer was commanded to guard them carefully. Upon receiving such orders, he put them in the inner cell and fastened their feet in the stocks. About midnight Paul and Silas were praying and singing hymns to God, and the other prisoners were listening to them. Suddenly there was such a violent earthquake that the foundations of the prison were shaken. At once all the prison doors flew open, and everybody's chains came loose (Acts 16:23-26).

This account reminds us that our praises will not only set us free, but also free those around us. Chains were broken and prison doors flew open as Paul and Silas prayed and sang. Scriptures teach us that worship brings not only deliverance and revelation, but also salvation. The jailer asked Paul and Silas: *"What must I do to be saved?"* If Paul and Silas had kept silent that day, souls would not have been saved. Deal with the Python spirit and boldly declare the praises of God wherever you are! Freedom requires constant vigilance!

7. The Spirit of Deafness and Muteness-
Resists Faith

When Jesus saw that a crowd was running to the scene, he rebuked the evil spirit. "You deaf and mute spirit," he said, "I command you, come out of him and never enter him again."
(Mark 9:25)

Confession has several meanings, one of which means that

we repeat and believe what someone else has already said. There is tremendous power in confession because we are saying what God has already said. Our songs of worship should be the echoes of heaven. Confession is an agreement with heaven and releases his kingdom upon the earth. Satan wants to blind us from these truths and mute our confession.

The god of this age has blinded the minds of unbelievers, so that they cannot see the light of the gospel of the glory of Christ, who is the image of God. (2 Corinthians 4:4)

We must unmute the sounds of heaven upon the earth. Our worship declares the glory of Christ and opens the eyes of faith.

8. The Spirit of Infirmity-
Resists Health

A woman was there who had been crippled by a spirit for eighteen years. She was bent over and could not straighten up at all. When Jesus saw her, he called her forward and said to her, "Woman, you are set free from your infirmity." Then he put his hands on her, and immediately she straightened up and praised God. (Luke 13:11-13)

Worship creates an environment for heaven to be released. The spirit of infirmity caused a woman to be crippled for eighteen years. I encourage people to command the spirit of infirmity to leave just like Jesus did in the book of Luke.

I recently heard a testimony of a man who was being hospitalized for weakness and confusion. Doctors were baffled because his all the tests they did came back positive and they could find nothing wrong with him. The man's son told him, "Dad, worship Jesus!" As the man began to praise God, all the color came back into his face and his strength returned.

Confronting Your Reality With Heaven

Worship confronts reality with the kingdom of God. When you feel under the weather, change the atmosphere with praise. If your reality is not heaven, and what you are experiencing is not what heaven is experiencing, your reality needs an invasion from heaven. Many Christians believe Jesus did miracles to prove that He was the Messiah. I tell people that Jesus did not come to show off, but to show us how to live. If Jesus commanded evil spirits to leave, then I will do the same.

We read in the Scriptures how Jesus commanded demons to leave and at other times caused the deliverance to happen by His presence. Worship is one of the best activities we can do to bring the presence of God. There is power in worship because God comes in our midst. The Father anointed Jesus with power and that same power lives in us.

God anointed Jesus of Nazareth with the Holy Spirit and power, and how he went around doing good and healing all who were under the power of the devil, because God was with him.
(Acts 10:38)

I pray that the body of Christ will continue to allow worship to create an atmosphere of healing and deliverance for all who gather in the name of Jesus.

Reflection

1. Satan questioned Jesus about His identity as the "Son of God." How does our identity affect our ability to worship and serve the LORD?

2. What tactic is Satan using most often attack you? The area of your identity, your strength, your hunger for God, your hope and vision or your value system?

3. What breaks the power of the spirit of Heaviness?

4. Does the spirit of Mammon ever affect our worship?

5. How did Paul and Silas respond when the spirit of Python attacked them?

Chapter 9

Our Spiritual Act of Worship

Some teachers in the body of Christ are changing the definition of the grace of God. Grace is taught as a license for sin instead of divine enablement for holy living. Jude warns:

For certain men whose condemnation was written about long ago have secretly slipped in among you. They are godless men, who change the grace of our God into a license for immorality and deny Jesus Christ our only Sovereign and Lord. (Jude 1:4)

Many in the church are denying Jesus as Lord, not in their words but in their actions. Jesus said, *"Why do you call me,*

'Lord, Lord,' and do not do what I say?" (Luke 6:46) We deny Jesus as Lord when we take His grace and turn it into a license for sin. Jesus has made a way for us to come into relationship with the Father through His blood. We are no longer sinners who need grace; we are the righteousness of God in Christ Jesus and have overcome the power of sin. The author of the letter to the Hebrews wrote:

We must pay more careful attention, therefore, to what we have heard, so that we do not drift away. For if the message spoken by angels was binding, and every violation and disobedience received its just punishment, how shall we escape if we ignore such a great salvation? (Hebrews 2:1-3)

We live in a society with many winds of teaching that can cause us to drift from our destination. It is time we pay more attention to what we have heard and not ignore our great salvation. This salvation is a gift that must be treasured and embraced because it was given to us with great love. Salvation also carries a responsibility on our part— a reasonable expectation on how we should live our lives. Covenant requires us to walk as a covenant partner with God by faith in Jesus Christ. *Though we are not saved by holy living, we live holy because we are saved.*

Our world around us is spewing defilement in every direction, like a broken sewage pipe. Satan's tactic is to spew defilement in our direction in hopes us of sweeping us away from our destination in God.

Then from his mouth the serpent spewed water like a river, to overtake the woman and sweep her away with the torrent.
(Revelation 12:15)

Defilement is a doorway to unclean spirits and bondage. As I counsel someone who is oppressed by something demonic, I usually look for the doorway through which the demonic oppression has come. When the one I am counseling remains bound, Jesus usually directs me to one of these areas.

1. **Un-forgiveness**
2. **Vows Made**
3. **Lies Believed**
4. **Personal Sin**
5. **Generational Sin (Iniquity)**
6. **Unhealed Emotional Wounds**

Thoughts and actions open doorways to demonic influence. When we hear sin knocking at the door, we must resist through the blood of Jesus. Doorways lead to highways, and not holding strong will lead to demonic strongholds. Repent from the above actions and confess your sins to one another to receive healing.

Ungodly desires lead to sinful habits that bring about destructive lifestyles. Many Christians live hopeless, helpless lives because they have given in to unclean living. They now have become a habitation to demons. Someone once asked the popular Bible teacher Derek Prince if a Christian can have a demon. He responded, *"A Christian can have whatever they want!"*

James reminds us *"...to keep oneself from being polluted by the world"* (James 1:27). I have seen documentaries about companies that have released waste into what were once life-giving streams. Our enemy is spewing pollution into our society seeking to poison life-giving streams of entertainment, laws, education and family.

One of the most pollutive movements that ever hit America was the sexual revolution in the 1960's. Satan knew something big was coming and produced this counterfeit awakening. The Jesus Movement soon followed and swept in millions of young Americans who were radical in their beliefs. What we see happening in America today is another sexual awakening. Satan is spewing pollution in every direction because he knows a second Jesus Movement is about to explode.

Grace Empowered Living

One of my favorite scriptures is found in John 6:29 where Jesus answered, *"The work of God is this: to believe in the one he has sent."* My work is to believe in Jesus, God's Son. This belief is now credited as righteousness to me or 'right standing with God.' *"Abram believed the Lord, and he credited it to him as righteousness"* (Genesis 15:6). My legal and favorable standing with God is credited to my belief in Jesus. Because of this free gift, how should I live?

Isaiah said that those who have set themselves apart for God would be given *"...a name better than sons and daughters"* (Isaiah 56:5). I cannot imagine a name any better than son or daughter! As we set ourselves apart for the LORD in our thoughts and actions, we will find our greatest joy. Our reasonable response to the sacrifice of the Lord Jesus is a holy life! Hear the words of Isaiah:

When you spread out your hands in prayer, I will hide my eyes from you; even if you offer many prayers, I will not listen. Your hands are full of blood; wash and make yourselves clean. Take your evil deeds out of my sight! Stop doing wrong, learn to do right! Seek justice, encourage the oppressed. Defend the cause of the fatherless, plead the case of the widow. "Come now, let us reason together," says the Lord. "Though your sins are like scarlet, they shall be as white as snow; though they are red as crimson, they shall be like wool. If you are willing and obedient, you will eat the best from the land. (Isaiah 1:15-19)

The Hebrew *sedagah* means 'to be righteous.' *Sedagah* is defined: as:

A legal term between God and mankind or relationship among people, stressing that the parties involved should be faithful to the expectation of one another. Denotes the fairness in the sense of what is good for all parties involved.' [16]

God is unswerving in fairness and I no longer want to live below His expectations for me. God has given me righteousness but also has right expectations of me. I desire a deeper walk with Christ and to be found worthy of this great salvation. Scriptures remind us to lift up holy hands to God. *"Therefore I want the men everywhere to pray, lifting up holy hands"* (1 Timothy 2:8).

Salvation is not based upon my good works, but neither is my relationship with God to be misunderstood. Sin is not an action: it is a power. Under the New Covenant I am free from the power of sin. I understand my part in the New Covenant and I am blessed! *"All the ways of the Lord are loving and faithful toward those who keep the demands of his covenant"* (Psalm 25:10).

The blood of Jesus empowers me over all the works of the devil, including sin! Jesus' blood empowers the righteous, but does not enable the wicked. Shame on those who believe for one second that God would send Jesus to enable us to continue sinning! Our lives should be examples of those empowered by grace. A person who is sinning is of the devil. Do not be deceived.

He who does what is sinful is of the devil, because the devil has been sinning from the beginning. The reason the Son of God appeared was to destroy the devil's work. (1 John 3:8)

We can never substitute passionate worship for holy living. A bird must have two wings to fly; passion is one wing and devotion to God is the other. A one-winged bird will never fly- it will merely flap around on the ground never reaching its heavenly destination. Paul reminds us what our spiritual act of worship really is:

---

[16] Ibid

Therefore, I urge you, brothers and sisters, in view of God's mercy, to offer your bodies as a living sacrifice, holy and pleasing to God—this is your spiritual act of worship. (Romans 12:1)

God has called us to offer our bodies as living sacrifices. In view of His mercy, we must live in the fear of the LORD, holy and pleasing to Him. True and proper worship defined.

Summoned By God

Every one who is part of the kingdom of God has been summoned. The Hebrew word for summoned is *qara*, which means:

To cry out, call; to name; to proclaim; pronounce, preach; to summon to court: is used to signify the act of naming, which is sometimes an assertion of sovereignty over the thing which is being named. Essentially denotes the specific message which is usually addressed to a specific recipient intended to elicit a specific response.[17]

When I think about being summoned, I think about jury duty. A summons demands a certain response from a certain person. There are three times in Isaiah in which God summons us by name.

1. *"Fear not, for I have redeemed you; I have summoned you by name; you are mine"* (Isaiah 43:1). Because we have been summoned by name, our response cannot be fear because we belong to Him. Hear Him call your name right now!

2. *"I will give you the treasures of darkness, riches stored in*

---

[17] Zodhiates, Spiros, and John R. Kohlenberger. *The Hebrew-Greek Key Study Bible: New International Version*. Chattanooga, TN: AMG Pub. 1996. 1549

secret places, so that you may know that I am the Lord, the God of Israel, who summons you by name" (Isaiah 45:3). He summons us to receive what we need in this season. You may be in this place of desperate provision. Hear Him call your name right now!

3. "For the sake of Jacob my servant, of Israel my chosen, I summon you by name and bestow on you a title of honor" (Isaiah 45:4). He summons us by name to restore us to a place of honor that we do not deserve.

As God has summoned us by name, He has also summoned us together. In the *One New Man Bible*, it says:

The Greek word ekklesia, which means a gathering of citizens called out from their homes into some public place. Implicit in Ekklesia is a summoning, so this is not just a collection of people, but people called out to a public meeting for a particular purpose.[18]

The church is a summoned group of people. We are not just a group of people crossing the street together when the light turns red! We have been summoned for a purpose for such a time as this. The *ekklesia* is prophesied to *"expand with such vigor and force that not even the powers of Hell can prevail!"*[19] Paul declares to the believers in Ephesus about God's purpose for the *ekklesia:*

His intent was that now, through the church, the manifold wisdom of God should be made known to the rulers and authorities in the heavenly realms, according to his eternal

18 Morford, William J. *The One New Man Bible: Revealing Jewish Roots & Power*. N.p.: n.p., n.d. Print.
19 Zodhiates, Spiros, and John R. Kohlenberger. *The Hebrew-Greek Key Study Bible: New International Version*. Chattanooga, TN: AMG Pub.1996. 1618

purpose that he accomplished in Christ Jesus our Lord.
(Ephesians 3:10-11)

We are not just called to gather, but to gather with an intended purpose to declare the wisdom of God to the world. Our journey as the *ecclesia*, or church, begins with summoning the name of the Lord Jesus. The Old Testament says, *"And everyone who summons the name of the Lord will be saved,"* (Joel 2:32) and the New Testament echoes this same verse in Acts 2:21, *"And everyone who calls on the name of the Lord will be saved."* (Acts 2:21). Summon the name of Jesus and let His salvation flow into your life.

As we worship we must receive our summons as well as summon the name of Jesus. Worship is one of the most unifying forces on the planet. Worship unites us vertically with heaven and horizontally with each other on earth.

The Key To Worship

A few days prior to the day Jesus was crucified, He entered Jerusalem to the sound of praise. The city was in an uproar in excitement and great expectation of what Jesus was about to do. We call this day Palm Sunday because the Bible says, *"(a) very large crowd spread their cloaks on the road, while others cut branches from the trees and spread them on the road"* (Matthew 21:8).

The crowds zealously threw down cloaks and branches before the Lord to celebrate His entrance into Jerusalem. The religious leaders of the day said to Jesus, *"Teacher, rebuke your disciples!"* (Luke 19:39). Sacrificial worshippers bring offense to religious observers. A football team can score a touchdown and the world can celebrate with shouting, jumping and dancing. A worshipper leader exclaims, "Give Jesus a shout of praise," and is rebuked as a fanatic!

Jesus responded to the religious leaders saying, **"I tell you... if they keep quiet, the stones will cry out"** (vs.40).

Scriptures tells us that even creation itself is groaning in anticipation of its soon coming freedom from the bondage of decay (Romans 8:21). Few, if any, in the crowd could have imagined what Jesus was about to do. Mankind's bondage to sin and decay was about to be extinguished through the blood of the Son of God.

The body of Christ should never make excuses for being too extreme in their worship and praise. I would rather err on the side of being too extravagant than being too conservative. I would rather offend man than offend God.

As Jesus continued into Jerusalem, *"(t)he crowds that went ahead of him and those that followed shouted, 'Hosanna to the Son of David, blessed is He who comes in the name of the Lord, Hosanna in the highest!'"* (Matthew 21:9)

The desperation of their praise is clearly seen in the word *hosanna*, which in Hebrew means *"save us"* (Ps. 118:25). *Hosanna* is cry of salvation from a desperate people to the One who can save them. The cry *hosanna* and the name of Jesus are both derived from the Hebrew word *yasa*, which means *"to save, rescue, deliver, help, preserve, give victory."*[20] Shouting *"Hosanna"* is a shout to Jesus!

The key to worship is to realize that Jesus Himself is our source of salvation. Maybe at the next worship service you attend you might not drag in some tree limbs and throw them at the altar along with your coats and jackets, but at least you more fully understand what it means to cry out *"Hosanna!"*

If we direct any of the credit of our own salvation to our own works, we are robbing Jesus of the glory He deserves. Worship flows out of a heart of gratitude. Gratitude is the response to a gift freely given, not earned or deserved.

Until we realize what we truly deserve, we will never appreciate what we have been given. *Hosanna* declares our need for someone to save us. Jesus's name means "Yahweh saves!"

---

[20] Zodhiates, Spiros, and John R. Kohlenberger. *The Hebrew-Greek Key Study Bible: New International Version*. Chattanooga, TN: AMG Pub.1996. 1522

Our praise is directed toward the Son of God and to the Father who sent Him. The psalmist declares:

Sing to the Lord a new song, for he has done marvelous things; his right hand and his holy arm have worked salvation for him.
(Psalm 98:1)

The Bible records that *"when Jesus entered Jerusalem, the whole city was stirred"* (Matthew 21:10). The translation of the word 'stirred' is derived from the Greek word *seio*. It means "to shake."[21] *Seio* is the root word of the English word 'seismic' and describes an event of enormous proportion. In Jerusalem on that day, their praise for their Redeemer was so exuberant that it was depicted by the same word that means a violent earthquake.

Palm Sunday is remembered as one of the greatest worship events of history. Those farther away exclaimed, *"'Who is this?' The crowds answered, 'This is Jesus, the prophet from Nazareth in Galilee'"* (Matthew 21:10-11). May our worship services cause outsiders to wonder, "Who is this that you are so exuberant about?"

Those who opposed Jesus stood on the outskirts of one of the greatest worship events of history baffled and discouraged. *"So the Pharisees said to one another, 'See, this is getting us nowhere. Look how the whole world has gone after Him!'"* (Matthew 21:19).

The power of worship is one of the greatest influences we can release on the earth. Worship will baffle and discourage our enemies while causing the world to go madly after Jesus! While we encourage radical worship at our gatherings, we must equally encourage radical worship in our lifestyles. Our greatest spiritual act of worship is to offer our bodies as living sacrifices holy and pleasing to God. We must live our lives fused with pure lifestyles and passionate worship releasing heaven wherever we go.

---

[21] Ibid. 1671

Reflection

1. The Hebrew word *segadah* is a legal term describing a relationship among people or between God and mankind stressing that the parties involved should be faithful to the expectation of one another. In your opinion, do you think most Christians understand what is expected of them in their relationship with God?

2. To be summoned assumes a certain _____ from a certain _____.

3. When Jesus entered Jerusalem on Palm Sunday, the entire city was stirred. What word is used to describe this event?

4. Define the word *hosanna* and how it is used in worship.

5. Each of us are summoned by God individually and summoned corporately as the church. What is the Greek word for church and what does it mean?

Chapter 10

Is Anyone Happy?

James asked the question, *"Is anyone happy?"* The response of happy people, James says, is for *"them [to] sing songs of praise."* (James 5:13) Worship is the by-product of happiness. If people are not worshipping, they are not happy; people are not happy because they do not know that God is for them and not against them. I like to begin all my worship sessions with this scripture:

What, then, shall we say in response to this? If God is for us, who can be against us? He who did not spare his own Son, but gave him up for us all—how will he not also, along with him, graciously give us all things? (Romans 8:31-32)

God's goodness toward me is confirmed by the fact that He gave up His own Son for me. It would be absurd for me to doubt his generosity. Imagine if I came to your house and you signed over your entire inheritance to me. You hand me the papers, hugging me and blessing me in the process. Should I feel any hesitation to ask for a glass of water on the way out?

Many times I believe God is in a good mood, but not necessarily toward me. Belief is the key to receiving. Doubt is defined as a

D.umb **O**.bservation **U**.ndermining **B**.asis **T**.ruth

Happiness comes through understanding and then fully embracing your place in God's heart. God's heart toward us is fully revealed to us by what Jesus has done. What should our response then be? Joyful, exuberant worship!

Why are so many gatherings in Jesus' name so somber and depressing? The congregation is probably in disbelief. Skepticism thrives in a somber atmosphere. Once this atmosphere is established, it will release more negativity. Atmospheres need to be kingdom atmospheres that create an environment of life, not death.

When our congregation gathers, we make this declaration corporately:

Anything God has done anywhere he can do here!
Anything God has done at any time he can do now!
Anything God has done through anyone he can do through me!

An atmosphere of faith is created by confession that flows out of a heart on fire for Jesus. Words carry atmosphere-changing power!

The Greenhouse Effect

Scientists have been working on ways to bring life to Mars, the fourth planet in our solar system. Mars is the next planet outside of Earth's orbit. As life can only exist on a planet with an atmosphere, many scientists proposed manufacturing and placing thousands of portable oxygen releasers on Mars. These oxygen releasers, over a long period of time, would create an atmosphere of life on the planet. Mars would become inhabitable and the people of Earth could begin a new life on a different planet!

God is seeking to bring life to His people on planet Earth. The atmosphere is the key to life. Scientists would call this the Greenhouse Effect. Green represents growth and health. House represents covering and protection. Effect represents an action that causes something is happening.

When we gather as the church, the greenhouse effect should be evident. A greenhouse is meant to be a place for tiny plants to grow and become fruitful. Its atmosphere enhances the effects of the sun upon the sprouts and causes them to grow more quickly and safely on their journey to maturity.

Satan loves to destroy the atmosphere of the church. Often he will tear down the greenhouse leaving the church open to the harsh environment of the world. Other times, Satan will install magnifying glass on the greenhouse, distorting the rays of the sun so that they are no longer nurturing but harmful. Instead of being blessed you get burned!

The core values that we carry determine the way the light of God's Son shines through us. If we are harsh to the bride of Christ, her heart will be shut down and made callous. If we are careless in preparing the bride of Christ to stand before her king, she will be unfit for service. We should examine our own hearts daily and determine how the light of Christ is shining through us. Jesus said that He was the door to the kingdom, but we are the windows. People cannot get into the kingdom by us but they can see into the kingdom through us.

Happy, Happy, Happy

The kingdom of God is modeled well in many areas of the world. One group that models the kingdom— sometimes even better than the church— is the Disney organization. The church can learn a lot from modeling after Disney in the areas where it looks like the kingdom of God.

1. Disney makes people happy

Disney is a major force in our society because they have wisely embraced the message that many in the church have failed to proclaim. God is in a radically good mood toward you and me. We should not be ashamed to smile in the kingdom. The most productive people on the planet are creative and happy people. They are driven by the joy and the ideas are that flowing from heaven into their hearts. I used to think that sober and serious was the state of mind in the kingdom, but the kingdom of God is a happy place. One third of the kingdom is joy. Happiness is a motivator that Christians need to embrace instead of avoid. Our Heavenly Father desires to fill the earth with sons and daughters through the proclamation of Jesus Christ as His Son. Jesus is the doorway to the kingdom, and His name unleashes the power of heaven. We must live the kingdom, as Paul wrote, *"For the kingdom of God is righteousness, peace and joy in the Holy Spirit"* (Romans 14:17).

2. Disney is not just a place, it's an Influence

Disney is a place to go, but is also an empire that is expanding. It's is a place that reaches out into the airwaves, influencing the minds of millions all over the world through music, film and television. Many Christians view heaven as a place to go after you die instead of a resource that is available to us in the present. Heaven is a place, but it is an empire that is supposed to be expanding and growing in influence.

3. Disney employs, attracts, and trains people

Disney is known to be one of the best places to work. It has usually been known to be family-friendly and the workers are trained to carry the vision. The kingdom of God needs to be the center of creativity. Here is where the problems of the world encounter the solution: God's Son, Jesus Christ. We must position ourselves in expectation of changing the world instead of positioning ourselves in expectation of the rapture.

4. Disney is all about fun and children

People look forward to going to Disneyland; I cannot imagine anyone going out of obligation. The greatest joy of parents is to see their children having fun. We must understand that the kingdom of God is fun as well and child friendly. Children easily enter into the supernatural and engage in the kingdom more than we realize. We recently had five children in our kids' church all have the same dream the night before church about being at a tea party. Our children's leader had been inspired as well to have a tea party that day. Parents just need to relax and become like a child; the kingdom is a place where children and parents have fun together.

4. Disney speaks to destiny not to their sins

Disney embraces and encourages the message that is missing in most of the church: to dream and fulfill their destiny. Unfortunately, when destiny and dreaming is pursued without an allegiance to the Lordship of Jesus in one's life, dreams will be shattered and destinies will be diverted. The church has put too much emphasis on sin, not on destiny. The message of hell should be plan B when people do not respond. I believe in hell and judgment, but plan A is that the goodness of God leads to repentance.

5. Disney is magical

People are willing to pay the ticket price and travel the distance for Disney because it is a magical place. People are attracted to a place that has a heartbeat for supernatural encounters and not just head knowledge. When the church becomes supernatural, it will become wealthy, not impoverished. The church will have long lines, not empty seats. The church should be magically supernatural, not spiritually dead. The church is a place where your dreams become reality because of what Jesus has done.

Stuck at 211

To see changes in the church, we must change the way we see God and each other. I heard statistics that 10% of churches say they want change, but only 3% really want change. In the end, maybe only 1%-2% are able to bring change to the way they do church.

Many believers are not willing to press through for change. Water at 212 degrees Fahrenheit experiences a transformation. Water at 211 degrees Fahrenheit remains in its current state. Just one degree makes a difference!

Are you at 211? Why not press through to the point of transformation? The kingdom of darkness will allow up to 211 and keep you satisfied with one degree short. Let a holy dissatisfaction overtake you and be transformed like water transforming into steam.

In our worship, we have authority to make declarations that will bring strength to the body of Christ. The prophet Isaiah reminds us of the need to declare encouragement through our praises:

Strengthen the feeble hands, steady the knees that give way; say to those with fearful hearts, "Be strong, do not fear; your God will come, he will come with vengeance; with divine retribution he will come to save you." (Isaiah 35:3-4)

When we began to receive the revelation that God is for us and not against us, *"Then will the lame leap like a deer, and the mute tongue shout for joy"* (Isaiah 35:6). The normal progression of healing is that the lame will crawl or the mute will talk. Isaiah declares that the lame man doesn't just walk; he leaps! The mute man doesn't just talk; he shouts! When we fully understand what God has done for us we will become fully engaged in worship. We cannot be satisfied with just walking and talking when we should be leaping and shouting.

Avoi*dance* or Abun*dance*?

The topic of dance as a form of worship is often not discussed. The church is more about avoidance than dance! There may be a dance team, but that is only for a specified group. Even calling the people on stage as the worship team can relieve the congregation from being the worship team. The scriptures do not relegate the job of worshipping to a few people in the congregation! The responsibility to praise and worship does not rest on the pastor or the worship leader; it is the responsibility of each person to offer up an individual sacrifice of praise to the LORD.

Everyone in the congregation is on the worship team and on the dance team. God sets apart a few people to lead in worship, but each of us must join the worship and dance team every time we gather together.

King David wrote, *"Let them praise his name with dancing and make music to him with timbrel and harp"* (Psalm 149:3). Again David wrote in Psalm 150:4, *"Praise him with timbrel and dancing, praise him with the strings and pipe."* Dancing is a normal response to great news!

I think about the end of World War II and the people flooding the streets with dancing to celebrate. The church has the greatest news and the greatest victory to celebrate! What is holding us back?

Scripture clearly demonstrates the need for dance as part of our worship. The Hebrew word *machool* refers to "whirling around in circular movements."[22] David danced before the LORD with all his might. Spinning is a form of worship.

The Hebrew word *chagag* means "to hold a festival, celebrate." [23] The Hebrew word *raqad* means "to skip, to leap about, to dance."[24] All these words are to be incorporated as part of our worship experience.

Too often worship is relegated to singing. In the Hebrew language, three words used to express praise involve dancing. Biblical worship always should include movement and body language. If the body of Christ desires abundance, they must dance!

God's Great Dance Floor

God will not have an end-time church that is cynical, depressed, religious, doubtful, or powerless. Our religious arguments with sinners will not bring revival. The joy of the LORD will be our strength and our greatest evangelical tool. Celebration not only fires us up to build the church, it strengthens the body of Christ and bonds us together.

After great defeats of a common enemy, there was great celebration. Moses led the people out of Egypt on the day of Passover. The people were commanded to place the blood of the lamb upon their doorposts as a sign of their deliverance. The Passover feast continued to the times of Jesus' day. God's Son not only celebrated the Passover, He fulfilled the Passover. Jesus was crucified on the day of this Feast and became the Lamb that would deliver mankind from their enemies.

---

22 Harris, R. Laird, Gleason L. Archer, and Bruce K. Waltke. *Theological Wordbook of the Old Testament*. Chicago: Moody, 1980. Print. 623

23 Zodhiates, Spiros, and John R. Kohlenberger. *The Hebrew-Greek Key Study Bible: New International Version*. Chattanooga, TN: AMG Pub.1996. 1933

24 Ibid. 2015

The people of Israel left Egypt on their way to the Promised Land. They were only three days out before Pharaoh decided to pursue and destroy them. The blood of the Passover lamb delivered them out of Pharaoh's hand, but the victory was not yet complete.

Many Christians stop at the cross in their worship. They sing about the blood but never move forward into the completed work that Jesus accomplished. Some of the most powerful experiences I have had in worship began as we sang about the blood of Jesus. The blood is the foundation on which we stand, but the victory wasn't complete until three days later at His resurrection.

When Yahweh parted the Red Sea three days after the Israelites left Egypt, He was painting a picture of what He would do fifteen hundred years later through His Son Jesus. The Red Sea crossing of the people of Israel is a prophetic picture to us fulfilled in the resurrection. Both events occurred three days after the blood of the Passover lambs was poured out, and both events declare our freedom from bondage.

When Pharaoh's horses, chariots and horsemen went into the sea, the LORD brought the waters of the sea back over them, but the Israelites walked through the sea on dry ground.
(Exodus 15:19)

On that day, the greatest army in the world was defeated and wiped off the face of the planet. The Israelites no longer had to fear the ones who had forced them into slavery. All of them were dead. Yahweh even had them float to shore from the bottom of the Red Sea so they could look at their limp bodies and see with their own eyes what God had done. This victory was not complete without a celebration!

Then Miriam the prophet, Aaron's sister, took a timbrel in her hand, and all the women followed her, with timbrels and dancing. Miriam sang to them: "Sing to Yahweh, for he is highly exalted. Both horse and driver he has hurled into the sea." (Exodus 15:20-21)

Miriam led the Israelites in the circle dance as a declaration of their joy and freedom they were experiencing through this victory. In the same way, during every gathering we should be dancing and whirling and spinning with joy because of the resurrection victory Jesus has won for us. It's time to hit the dance floor!

The Victory Dance

About five hundred years later, the people of Israel were again being tormented by an enemy. The Philistines were stationed in the Israelites' cities in garrisons, taunted their authority, and belittled the people of Israel. God sent one young man, David, to slay their enemy's greatest warrior and drive them out. After David killed Goliath, the people celebrated with dancing!

When the men were returning home after David had killed the Philistine, the women came out from all the towns of Israel to meet King Saul with singing and dancing, with joyful songs and with timbrels and lyres. (1 Samuel 18:6-8)

Every great victory should be followed by a great celebration. Every great celebration must include dancing. The Israelites danced because David had slain their enemies! Dancing is a declaration of freedom— no more shackles, no more chains— I am free!

When God Himself throws a party, there is music and dancing. God Himself is rejoicing over you. You are His precious child, and the world would never believe how much God delights in His prodigals who have returned to Him. Jesus has made the way through His own blood to bring you back into the Father's house. The greatest story of Our Heavenly Father's love is seen in the story of the prodigal son.

"Bring the fattened calf and kill it. Let's have a feast and celebrate. For this son of mine was dead and is alive again; he was lost and is found." So they began to celebrate. Meanwhile, the older son was in the field. When he came near the house, he heard music and dancing. (Luke 15:23-25)

When the father celebrated the return of the prodigal son, he turned up the music and everyone hit the dance floor! The only one not celebrating was the older son who worked hard but never realized all that was really his in his father's house.

Do you realize all that is yours because of what Jesus has purchased for you? Are you receiving it freely or are you still trying to work hard for it? The love of God is a gift and is coming at us at full throttle. We must learn to receive His love in its fullness and not ever base it upon what we have or have not done. Join in the celebration that you are now part of God's family. He sings, dances and longs for His people to join Him!

(The LORD) Yahweh your God is with you, the Mighty Warrior who saves. He will take great delight in you; in His love He will no longer rebuke you, but will rejoice (dance, spin, circle) over you with singing. (Zephaniah 3:17)

King David danced unashamedly before the LORD and he had a response for his critics. Decide today how you will answer those who will be offended by your worship. Let David's words shape your response:

It was before the Lord, who chose me... when he appointed me ruler over the Lord's people Israel—I will celebrate before the Lord. I will become even more undignified than this...
(2 Samuel 6:21-22)

121

David rejoiced in an undignified manner because he knew that he was chosen by the LORD to rule. His critics merely caused him to commit to an even more radical lifestyle of worship. I hope you as well will count it an honor to begin embracing undignified worship. The power of worship is invading earth and let it bulldoze every barrier hindering you from entering the fullness of God in you life!

Reflection

1. Worship is a by-product of happiness. Has the church done a good job of promoting happy people? What could we learn from the Disney Corporation whose mission statement is "To make people happy?"
2. What is the danger of calling the people on stage the worship team or the people on the platform the dance team?
3. Do you view celebration as a command? When God commands celebration as part of our lives should we obey in the same way we obey the Ten Commandments?
4. Why do our gathering times as the church resist dancing? What would happen if everyone hit the dance floor ever time we gathered in Jesus' name?
5. How does it feel to know that God Himself dances over you? Have you ever been danced over before?

Other Books by Christopher Monaghan

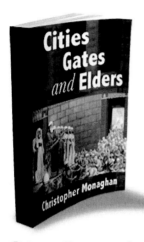

Cities, Gates and Elders answers the question of why Jesus told Peter, "...upon this rock I will build my church; and the gates of hell shall not prevail against it" (Matthew 16:18). The disciples of Jesus understood that the gates were gateways in which the elders of the city would sit and judge. The decisions made at these gates had authoritative power over regions. Jesus was saying that the decisions made in hell would not prevail against the decisions made on earth by His people.

If you were to open up a Hebrew dictionary, you would discover the first word in Hebrew is father. The Hebrew language begins with the most important word you will ever need to know. The book *Heaven's Dynasty* rediscovers the Father emphasis each of us need to have in our daily lives and the understanding of how to pass on the generational blessing as God did Himself to His Son. You will discover how to understand the New Testament Kingdom from a Jewish perspective.

about
the author

Chris Monaghan and his wife, Debbie, live near Richmond, Indiana, U.S.A. Chris and Debbie are the Senior Leaders of a group of believers in the Richmond area called Gateway Vineyard Fellowship. They focus on changing the atmosphere of their city through worship, teaching and humanitarian acts. Gateway seeks to create a movement centered on revival that flows out of our new identity in Jesus as sons and daughters in the kingdom of God. Chris and Debbie expect supernatural happenings whenever and wherever the body of Christ gathers together and regularly see physical and emotional healings take place. They also serve as coordinators for Family Foundations International and promote the Ancient Paths Seminars in their region. Chris and Debbie have five children: four boys and one girl.

Made in United States
North Haven, CT
18 October 2022